Elements in Religion and Monotheism
edited by
Paul K. Moser
Loyola University Chicago
Chad Meister
Affiliate Scholar, Ansari Institute for Global Engagement with Religion, University of Notre Dame

SEEKING MONOTHEISM IN CHINESE RELIGIONS

Huaiyu Chen
Arizona State University

Shaftesbury Road, Cambridge CB2 8EA, United Kingdom

One Liberty Plaza, 20th Floor, New York, NY 10006, USA

477 Williamstown Road, Port Melbourne, VIC 3207, Australia

314–321, 3rd Floor, Plot 3, Splendor Forum, Jasola District Centre, New Delhi – 110025, India

103 Penang Road, #05–06/07, Visioncrest Commercial, Singapore 238467

Cambridge University Press is part of Cambridge University Press & Assessment, a department of the University of Cambridge.

We share the University's mission to contribute to society through the pursuit of education, learning and research at the highest international levels of excellence.

www.cambridge.org
Information on this title: www.cambridge.org/9781009478540

DOI: 10.1017/9781009164443

© Huaiyu Chen 2025

This publication is in copyright. Subject to statutory exception and to the provisions of relevant collective licensing agreements, no reproduction of any part may take place without the written permission of Cambridge University Press & Assessment.

When citing this work, please include a reference to the DOI 10.1017/9781009164443

First published 2025

A catalogue record for this publication is available from the British Library

ISBN 978-1-009-47854-0 Hardback
ISBN 978-1-009-16531-0 Paperback
ISSN 2631-3014 (online)
ISSN 2631-3006 (print)

Cambridge University Press & Assessment has no responsibility for the persistence or accuracy of URLs for external or third-party internet websites referred to in this publication and does not guarantee that any content on such websites is, or will remain, accurate or appropriate.

Seeking Monotheism in Chinese Religions

Elements in Religion and Monotheism

DOI: 10.1017/9781009164443
First published online: April 2025

Huaiyu Chen
Arizona State University
Author for correspondence: Huaiyu Chen, Huaiyu.Chen@asu.edu

Abstract: In the nineteenth and early twentieth centuries, numerous Western missionaries were involved in debating the existence of God in various religious texts and practices in ancient China. Drawing on both the rising philological scholarship in Europe and their own field experience in China, the Western missionaries examined the idea of God, the Thearch, and Heaven as the Supreme Being in the spiritual life and ritual activities of the Chinese people. From the Christian perspective, they attempted to identify the original belief in one God in ancient China in order to convert their Chinese audience. Furthermore, they addressed the issue of monotheism in the broader Asian context by suggesting the universal monotheistic degeneration from Persia to China across Asia continent.

Keywords: monotheism, God, Truth, China, degeneration

© Huaiyu Chen 2025

ISBNs: 9781009478540 (HB), 9781009165310 (PB), 9781009164443 (OC)
ISSNs: 2631-3014 (online), 2631-3006 (print)

Contents

1 Introduction   1

2 Discovering the Thearch/God in Ancient Chinese Civilizations   10

3 Monotheism and Polytheism: From Ancient Religion to State Religion   26

4 Chinese Monotheism along the Silk Road and Indo-European Civilizations   37

5 From Monotheism to Polytheism in Chinese History   45

6 Chinese Religions: The Protestant Heritage in the Twentieth and Twenty-First Centuries   54

Bibliography   60

1 Introduction

1.1 The Issue and Significance

This Element relates the history of Western Protestant missionary writings about Chinese beliefs and religions from the standpoint of their Christian background in the nineteenth and early twentieth centuries. It investigates the historical and cultural context in which the Westerners came to terms with Chinese divine beings and gods when they arrived in China, which was, at that time, a collapsing traditional Asian empire. On the one hand, the Catholic missionaries continued the Jesuit tradition of seeking the historical roots of the Abrahamic "One God" in Chinese religions. On the other hand, the Protestant missionaries reinterpreted the Chinese pantheon and beliefs from the perspective of Protestant Christianity. With broader engagement with Asia in the nineteenth century, these Western missionaries also attempted to trace the theological and religious connections between China and West Asia, especially Persia, in light of the unilineal evolution theory of civilization. Many of the issues these missionaries addressed regarding Chinese religions laid the foundation for the modern study of Chinese religions and even East Asian religions. This Element analyzes this crucial yet underdeveloped chapter in the contemporary intellectual history of theology and faith across the Eurasian continent.

The study of Chinese religions is now often regarded as part of Chinese studies, or East Asian studies, that are classified as area studies or international studies in the contemporary college curricula in the United States. With the development of postcolonial and postmodern theories, the critical evaluation of the formation of the discipline in Europe and the United States has led to more nuanced investigations into the historical, cultural, and ideological contexts in which certain important subjects and themes were developed at the formative stage of the discipline. Contemporary scholars are now beginning to interrogate from different perspectives the definitions of many terms in the study of Chinese religions. Today very few scholars would use the term "Chinese religion" rather than "Chinese religions" to describe the spiritual reality in China, given that most scholars now view China as a multi-ethnic, multi-lingual, and multi-religious nation. Though the current state government of China only recognizes the legal status of five religions (Buddhism, Daoism, Islam, Catholicism, and Protestant Christianity), China is a vast nation with numerous other types of beliefs, rituals, and practices. Multiple ethnic groups and communities have lived their own religious lives on the ground or in the closet, using their languages, worshipping their gods, reading their texts, and performing rituals.

Nevertheless, monotheism as a modern concept and a Western construction has been a significant issue in the study of Chinese religious traditions since the seventeenth century. Given the contemporary reflexive scholarship, decolonizing knowledge has become a trend in some modern humanities disciplines. In dealing with monotheism in Chinese religions, we cannot separate it from the larger historical and cultural context behind the rise of religious studies as a modern humanities discipline. Guy C. Stroumsa attributed the rise of the modern approach to religious phenomena to three major historical events. The first was the Great Discoveries that brought the people and religions of the New and Old worlds, especially the Americas and South and East Asia, to light; the second was the Renaissance, which generated the Western interest in antiquity and the growth of modern philology that led to the publication of major religious texts from various classical and "oriental" languages; the third was the religious wars that took place across Western Europe in the wake of the Reformation, leading Europeans to turn to the non-Abrahamic religions in the Orient.[1] Tomoko Masuzawa notes that both anthropology and oriental studies played a significant role in the introduction of numerous religious traditions beyond Europe.[2] In many publications on religions that appeared in the eighteenth and nineteenth centuries, Christianity was first listed in opposition to paganism and idolatry and was then labeled as a universal religion, unlike many other religions such as Confucianism, Daoism, Shintoism, and Brahmanism that were classified as national religions.[3] Whether or not our understanding of Chinese religions is Eurocentric or Christianity-centric, we have inherited numerous terms and concepts from those forerunners who gave birth to the field of Chinese religions, especially Western missionaries.

Contemporary scholars in Chinse religious studies often face multidimensional challenges, such as the sources and fieldwork, academic training, and cultural, ethnic, and linguistic backgrounds. When they attempt to dialogue with their predecessors in the field, they might share some common ground with these forerunners, including the use of some concepts and terms developed by these forerunners, even though these concepts and terms are historically imbued with ideology. For example, the words such as "Buddhism," "Confucianism,"

---

[1] G. C. Stroumsa, *A New Science: The Discovery of Religion in the Age of Reason* (Cambridge, MA: Harvard University Press, 2010), 5–6.
[2] T. Masuzawa, *The Invention of World Religions, or How European Universalism Was Preserved in the Language of Pluralism* (Chicago: University of Chicago Press, 2005), 15–18.
[3] For example, R. Adam claimed that there were four major systems of religion: Judaism, Paganism, Christianity, and Mohammedism; see his *The Religious World Displayed* (Edinburgh: James Ballantyne for Longman, Hurst, Rees, and Orme, 1808); W. S. Lilly categorized six major religious traditions in the *Sacred Books of the East* into national or tribal religions and universal religions. Buddhism and Islam were regarded as universal religions, along with Christianity. However, Zoroastrianism, Confucianism, Daoism, and Brahmanism were listed as national religions; see Lilly, *Ancient and Modern Thought* (London: Chapman and Hall, 1885), 108–109.

and "Daoism" were invented in the nineteenth century and are believed to have appeared out of the Christian missionaries' assumptions based on their thoughts on Christianity. Confucianism as a term was invented by the missionaries because they thought that it was a philosophical and moral system centered on Confucius, which was similar to Christianity as a religion, centered on Christ. The Christian missionaries saw Buddhism as a system centered on the Buddha – though they thought it should be called Dharmism since the Dharma, the teachings of the Buddha, was the center of this tradition in its early stages. Similarly, in Christian missionary writings, Daoism was once called "Laoism" as a system centered on Laozi (Old Master) and Islam used to be called Muhammadism, a religion based on Muhammad.

As a modern humanities discipline, religious studies first appeared as comparative religions in Europe, focusing on the comparative studies of Christianity and other religious traditions. Then the history of religions appeared as an alternative approach to the religious traditions across the world. While modern scholars from Europe turned to study other religious traditions, they first examined some key themes that they were more familiar with in European history, such as God, the national religion, the state religion, and death and the afterlife. European scholars wondered if there was one true God in traditional China, a national religion for the Chinese nation, a state religion for the Chinese state, and death and afterlife in the Chinese religions.

The concern of many Western missionaries and scholars in Europe and America in the nineteenth century when dealing with non-European religions was with monotheism and polytheism. Regarding China, the Western missionaries attempted to ascertain whether monotheism had already existed in ancient China, because if it had, it might lay the foundation for the Chinese people's acceptance of Christianity as monotheistic (Christ as the only true God). For Christian missionaries, all doctrines such as ontology, eschatology, truth, creation, and salvation lead to the ultimate question about God. Therefore, looking for the one, true God or making sense of God, or the gods, became a central issue in the missionary understanding of Chinese religions. In brief, these missionaries understood the history of Chinese religions or teachings in the framework of Christian time. For them, if there was a tradition of a one, true God in ancient China, it would mean that this idea is universal and China could fit into the time framework of Christian theology.

The sources in this book are mainly drawn from the published writings of the nineteenth-century missionaries to China. Although the Catholic missionaries, especially the Jesuits, provided the basis for understanding Chinese religions, the Protestant missionaries produced far richer writings on Chinese philosophies and religions, based on both their experiences in the field and their reading. Unfortunately, in the nineteenth century modern archaeology was not yet well-developed in China and the oracle bones and bronze inscriptions had yet to become significant sources for understanding ancient Chinese religions. Once archaeological excavations began to take place, they changed our understanding of religious life in ancient China significantly.[4] For example, the discussion of the Great One (*Taiyi*) who gave birth to water began to flourish once the relevant text was discovered from the Guodian tomb, but it is completely missing from the writings of those missionaries.[5] Nevertheless, Western missionaries left numerous writings and records about China. As Anna Johnston noted, "British Protestant missionaries were prolific writers. Diaries, reports, letters, memoirs, histories, ethnographies, novels, children's books, translations, grammars, and many more kinds of texts spilled from their pens."[6] She emphasized that these texts are crucial to understanding the cross-cultural encounters. Indeed, the Protestant missionaries in China sent numerous reports and letters back to their home churches, addressing various mission and life issues and telling their stories in China. For example, Jane R. Edkins (1838–1861) sent many letters to her father from China. After her death, her father wrote and published her biography, along with her letters.[7] These letters become important sources of understanding her life in China and her encounters with Chinese culture. Some of the letters documented how her husband, Joseph Edkins (1823–1905), taught Chinese Christians theology and studied Chinese Buddhism and Daoism. The London Missionary Society also issued many publications for its members and subscribers, among which were the monthly *Chronicle*, quarterly *Missionary Sketches*, and yearly *Reports to the Directors*.

In Asia, the Protestant missionaries published a large number of pamphlets, tracts, journals, magazines, and translations of the Bible. Many debates on the translations of the Bible appeared in the missionary magazine *The Chinese Repository* in the 1840s following a missionary conference in 1843. More discussions were published in the *Chinese Recorder and Missionary Journal*. Many Protestant missionaries published their essays, letters, reports, and

---

[4] M. Poo, *In Search of Personal Welfare* (Albany: State University of New York, 1998).
[5] K. Holloway, *Guodian: The Newly Discovered Seeds of Chinese Religious and Political Philosophy* (Oxford: Oxford University Press, 2008); M. Puett, *To Become a God* (Cambridge, MA: Harvard University Press, 2002), 160–164.
[6] A. Johnston, *Missionary Writing and Empire: 1800–1860* (Cambridge: Cambridge University Press, 2003), 3. For a general introduction to the sources on Christianity in China, see R. G. Tiedemann ed., *Christianity in China, Volume Two: 1800–Present* (Leiden: Brill, 2010), 1–92.
[7] J. R. Edkins, *Chinese Scenes and People* (London: James Nisbet, 1863).

articles in these publications. The editorial and conference committees from the missionary conferences in Shanghai in 1877, 1890, and 1907 published the records or reports of these conferences. Some missionaries also published a large number of tracts and pamphlets in Chinese while working in China. William Muirhead (1822–1900), a London Mission Society missionary who spent more than half a century in Shanghai, published a Chinese book in Japan in 1879, with a concise introduction to five religions in China – Confucianism, Buddhism, Daoism, Islam, and Protestant Christianity. Most of these pamphlets were tracts targeting Chinese Christian audience; they were full of simple and concise statements rather than articulated discussions. Nevertheless, the Protestant missionaries often published lengthy books to elaborate on their field experience in China and their views on important issues about Chinese thought, geography, religions, and political institutions. Many of these missionaries later became Sinologists who engaged with the European and American scholarship on modern oriental studies or religious studies. Their discussions on Chinese religions combined both their Protestant Christian perspective and the scholarly orientation of modern humanities. Therefore, in this Element I will pay more attention to the writings published by Protestant missionaries that elaborated and articulated their ideas and discussions on monotheism in China in the context of both the intellectual history of Christianity in China and the history of modern humanities.

More specifically, some of the British and American Protestant missionaries became the first generation of Sinologists to occupy faculty positions in British and American higher education institutions. My analysis will pay special attention to those missionaries-turned Sinologists for their contributions to the study of Chinese religions as a new field in the late nineteenth and early twentieth centuries, because they bridged not only the gap between the Christian theology and Chinese thought but also the gap between the religious studies as a new discipline in modern humanities and the oriental studies that denoted the European and American understanding of the so-called oriental civilizations and religions. While dealing with the non-Abrahamic religions based on newly uncovered manuscripts and artifacts, the Western forerunners of religious studies often raised the issues on key concepts in Abrahamic religions, such as monotheism.

This study aims to shed new light on the rise of Chinese religious studies as part of modern humanities in the nineteenth century and its Western and Chinese historical and cultural context. It also offers a new global perspective on the cultural encounters between the Westerners and Asian religions, philosophies, and societies in the nineteenth and early twentieth centuries. Finally, hopefully it will invoke more discussions on modern colonialism, imperialism, and nationalism by focusing on religion and philosophy.

1.2 The Structure

Section 2 examines the Westerners' intellectual journey of discovering the Thearch/God in ancient Chinese civilizations. For Christian missionaries, all doctrines such as ontology, eschatology, truth, creation, and salvation lead to the ultimate question of God. Looking for the true God or making sense of the gods became a central question in the missionary understanding of Chinese religions. Since the eighteenth and nineteenth centuries, the forerunners of the study of Chinese religions, especially Jesuit and Protestant missionaries, started asking if there was a God in the ancient Chinese belief systems. When Jesuits such as Matteo Ricci (1552–1610) and Guilio Aleni (1582–1649) came to China, they encountered seventeenth-century Neo-Confucianism. The Neo-Confucian thinkers directly exposed these Jesuits to the Great Ultimate (*Taiji*) concept as the origin of myriad things. However, by tracing the historical roots of the concept of the Ultimate in Chinese civilization, these Jesuits attempted to find the similarity between the Catholic God and the Thearch (*Shangdi*, Lord of the Heaven or the Sovereign on High) in ancient Chinese tradition, not the Great Ultimate (*Taiji*). These missionaries also argued that some Confucian thinkers believed in an immortal soul. However, when they read the Neo-Confucian writings, they found that the Neo-Confucian thought did not represent the original, "pure" Confucianism in ancient China. Therefore, these Jesuits attempted to identify the Thearch in ancient China with the God in Catholicism.

Western missionaries realized that the Thearch and Heaven held absolute power and ultimate authority in the Chinese Empire. Through the ages, the Chinese state developed a set of rites for offering sacrifices to Heaven to receive rewards and blessings. The missionaries began to link this religious system to the European concept of a state religion. Even before the first Protestant missionary, Robert Morrison (1782–1834), arrived in China in 1807, the British ministers tried to identify the religious ideas and practices carried out in the court of the Chinese empire as the state religion. As early as 1795, the British scholar William Winterbotham (1763–1829) proposed that the Chinese state religion was kind of primitive worship that could be found in the practices of the emperor, officials, and gentlemen (Confucian *junzi*). Furthermore, he identified the object of this worship as the Thearch (*di*), a free, intelligent Being and an all-powerful, avenging, and rewarding Spirit. He explained that over the ages, the Chinese emperors, as the high priests, all worshipped this Being. After Morrison came to China, he also became interested in the idea of a state religion in China. In 1834, he published an essay claiming that the Chinese state religion did not have doctrines for teaching, learning, or believing. He noted that this state religion included a set of rites and ceremonies, and it was mainly a bodily service. He pointed out that the state code of rituals institutionalized this Chinese state religion. However, as an increasing number of British missionaries came to China, they began to debate the question of a state religion in China – a debate that also continued among the other missionaries who came to China in the late nineteenth century.

Section 3 addresses the Western missionaries' rediscovery of monotheism in the what were known as the "Three Teachings" (Buddhism, Confucianism, and Daoism) in China. Some of the critical issues in the writings of the Western missionaries about Chinese religions were connected to their understanding of monotheism and polytheism. The study of the ancestral cult and ancestral sacrifice also led to studying the ideas about death, the afterlife, and immortality. The missionaries' concerns about death, life, and afterlife in Chinese religions nevertheless came from their understanding of eschatology in Christianity. In 1859, William Dean suggested that Confucianism was the state religion in China and that it was a kind of theism, despite the fact that Confucius did not recognize God or immortality. The idea of Confucianism as the state religion of China flourished among Western missionaries in the nineteenth century, with filial piety and the ancestral cult as their main concerns. Joseph Edkins (1823–1905) suggested that Confucius and Mencius followed monotheism because they focused on ancestral cults but remained silent about traditional astrology, five-phase philosophy, and other folk beliefs. He also noted that Liezi as a "Laoist" (Daoist) thinker believed that there was a God in the world and the *Book of Liezi* recorded many dialogues between Liezi and God. Many missionaries addressed the idea of immortality, a crucial issue deeply rooted in the Christian discourse of monotheism, as it appeared in Buddhism, Confucianism, and Daoism. J. Dyer Ball connected the ancestral cult in ancient Chinese religion with the idea of the soul's immortality, which may have paved the way for accepting the Buddhist concepts of heaven and paradise.

Section 4 examines how the missionaries discussed Chinese monotheism along the Silk Road and built a connection between it and Indo-European civilizations. The nineteenth century witnessed the growing interest of European scholars in non-Abrahamic religions across Asia. Many missionaries seemed to believe that numerous religious traditions in Asia shared the theory of revelation, and that there might have been a unilinear development of religious traditions across the continent. Moreover, they assumed that the ancestors of a number of philosophical and religious traditions in East Asia could be found in some of the more ancient traditions in West Asian civilizations, such as Babylon and Persia. To prove these assumptions, they turned to Indo-European historical philology and comparative religions.

Western explorers and archaeologists discovered and collected a large number of manuscripts and inscriptions from various parts of Asia. The scholarship on these manuscripts and notes uncovered along the Silk Road revealed various religious traditions of Asia, both living and dead, such as Zoroastrianism, Mazdaism, Manichaeism, Nestorianism, and the more well-known traditions, Buddhism and Judaism. In attempting to spread the new knowledge about these traditions and respond to Western readers' growing interest, Friedrich Max Müller (1823–1900) launched the enterprise of compiling the fifty-volume work, *Sacred Books of the East*. One of the most critical contributors was Joseph Edkins, a prolific Sinologist who had spent many years in China as a missionary. Edkins published many works that discussed Chinese and Persian religions' shared origins in light of Indo-European historical philology and comparative religions. He was particularly interested in whether there was an indigenous monotheism in ancient China and Persia. He attempted to build connections between the Chinese Thearch and the Persian Ahuramazda, and between China's six divinities and Persia's six ancient gods of water, wood, fire, metal, earth, and animals. Furthermore, Edkins traced the Chinese religion back to 3000 BCE Persia because he believed that he had discovered some common features in the ancient Chinese and Persian religions: dualism in the Chinese classic the *Book of Changes*, and dualism in Persian Zoroastrianism; offerings and sacrifices to the high mountains in ancient China and Persia; the five elements in both Persian and Chinese philosophies; and the twelve constellations in Babylonian tradition and zodiac theory in China. His study benefited from James Darmesteter's (1849–1894) work on the old Persian text *Avesta*, but he discussed the impact of Zoroastrianism in China and Japan. Hampden Coit Dubose (1845–1910), an American Baptist missionary active in China, continued Edkins's discussions on the internal connections among the different religious traditions in Asia. He further traced the origins of dualism in Manichaeism and its association with Buddhism and Daoism. Other missionaries were also interested in connecting the Chinese religions to those of South and West Asia.

Chapter Four investigates how missionaries developed the theory of motheism's degeneration into polytheism in Chinese history. Matteo Ricci first presented the theory that the Chinese religious tradition began with monotheism, but later it experienced a process of degeneration that led to polytheism. Some Protestant Christian missionaries echoed this idea. In the late nineteenth century, many missionaries began to discuss the degeneration of Chinese religion and mainly focused on the binary of the true God and idolatry in ancient Chinese beliefs. William Muirhead believed that the Chinese people had their own wisdom, philosophies, and speculations in ancient times. Later, however, their beliefs and imagination made them ignorant of the true God. He argued that Daoism was later mixed with idolatry and superstitions, and it was gradually distorted, while Confucian philosophy was also modified by idolatry such as ancestral worship. Arthur Evans Moule (1836–1918) also suggested an ancient religious tradition in addition to what he referred to as the "three sects" (Buddhism, Confucianism, and Daoism) that preserved ancient worship. But, it gradually declined into polytheism. Jas Johnston (1819–1905) argued that Confucianism and Buddhism appeared as pure religions but later they also fell into idolatry worship. Many other missionaries such as William A. P. Martin (1827–1916), James Dyer Ball (1847–1919), William Milne (1785–1822), William E. Soothill (1861–1935), and Hampden Coit DuBose had similar ideas. Some approached the issue from the philological perspective by studying Chinese classics, while others approached it from their fieldwork by investigating the religious experience of ordinary people in their contemporary period.

Section 6 serves as the concluding chapter, summarizing the main discussions from the previous chapter and developing further theoretical implications. It will focus on decolonizing the missionary knowledge of Chinese religions and analyzing the ways that Western missionaries laid the foundation for the modern study of Chinese religions, while at the same time, imbuing it with Christian ideology. In particular, this section contextualizes how Western missionaries interpreted Chinese religions in the modern political and intellectual milieu of the early twentieth century. It analyzes the debates on the nature of Confucianism and its relations with Chinese national and cultural identity; for example, one question is whether Confucianism was a state religion, a national religion, or a world religion. In other words, the missionaries were concerned about the positions of Chinese religions in China, Asia, and the world. Behind these debates, there were a series of political and religious transformations in China. Protestant Christianity's monotheism reflected the Christian value system as the only truth, which, along with Western imperialism, challenged the declining Chinese empire in the early twentieth century. In 1905, the Qing empire abandoned the civil examination system, and Confucianism lost its role as the cornerstone in the education of Chinese students and in preparing them to serve in the government. But the idea of Confucianism as the state religion impacted the Chinese intellectuals after the collapse of the Qing empire when China moved into the Republican era. Therefore, this chapter will also address the issue of monotheism in Chinese religions in the historical context of imperialism, colonialism, and nationalism in the early twentieth century.

2 Discovering the Thearch/God in Ancient Chinese Civilizations

2.1 Introduction

The Abrahamic religions have a long history in China. Some priests of the Church of the East, or the Luminous Teaching (Jingjiao), travelled across Central Asia along the Silk Road and arrived in Chang'an, the capital of the Tang empire, in 635. The Tang emperor declared that a church would be built where the believers could practice their religion. Monotheism and other essential doctrines such as the Trinity, Jesus's resurrection, and the immortal soul were introduced to China through the literary texts and stone monument inscriptions of this church.[8] Two other Abrahamic religions, Judaism and Islam, also arrived in China in the Tang dynasty (618–907), though not as early as the Church of the East.[9] The followers of these religious traditions did not translate many texts into the Chinese language, nor did their communities convert many Chinese followers. Mostly, they remained as foreign churches serving immigrants from West and Central Asia. These foreign immigrants often arrived in China as merchants or refugees, without necessarily having an articulated plan for preaching their religions.[10] Nevertheless, we should not assume that their monotheism was entirely unknown to the Chinese.

With the arrival of the Jesuit missionaries in China in the seventeenth century, the situation completely changed. These Jesuits aimed at converting the Chinese and expanding Catholicism in the Chinese empire. They faced the challenge of Confucianism, the dominant ideology at that time. Although they

---

[8] Y. Saeki, *The Nestorian Documents and Relics in China* (Tokyo: The Toho Bunkawa Gakuin, The Maruzen Company Ltd., 1951); I. Gillman and H.-J. Klimkeit, *Christians in Asia before 1500* (Ann Arbor: University of Michigan Press, 1999); P. Pelliot, *L'inscription nestorienne de Si-ngan-fu*, edited with supplements by A. Forte (Kyoto: Scuola di Studi sul l'Asie Orientale, Paris: College de France, Institut des Hautes Etudes Chinoises, 1996); H. Chen, "The Connection between Nestorian and Buddhist Texts in Late Tang China," in Roman Malek ed., *The Church of the East in China and Central Asia* (Sankt Augustin: Institut Monumenta Serica, 2006), 93–113; L. Tang, *A Study of the History of Nestorian Christianity in China and Its Literature in Chinese* (Frankfurt/M: Peter Lang, 2002); R. Malek, ed., *Jingjiao: The Church of the East in China and Central Asia* (Monumenta Serica Institute, Sankt Augustin, Nettetal: Steyler Verlag, 2006); M. Nicolini-Zani, *The Luminous Way to the East: Texts and History of the First Encounter of Christianity with China* (Oxford: Oxford University Press, 2022).

[9] Some missionaries called Islam "Mahometanism"; see G. W. Clarke, "The Introduction of Mahometanism into China," *The Chinese Recorder and Missionary Journal* (June, 1886), 269–271; (August, 1886), 294–296.

[10] N. Sims-Williams, "Sogdian and Turkish Christians in the Turfan and Tun-huang Manuscripts," in A. Cadonna ed., *Turfan and Tun-huang the Texts: Encounter of Civilization on the Silk Road* (Firenze: Leo S. Olschki, 1992), 43–61; R. C. Foltz, *Religions of the Silk Road* (New York: St. Martin's Press, 1999); F. Grenet, "Religious Diversity among Sogdian Merchants in Sixth-Century China: Zoroastrianism, Buddhism, Manichaeism, and Hinduism," *Comparative Studies of South Asia, Africa and the Middle East*, 27: 2 (2007), 463–478; M. Loewe, "The Jewish Presence in Imperial China," *Jewish Historical Studies*, 30 (1988), 1–20.

had already touched on the doctrinal conflict over the concept of God with their Chinese audience, they seemed to be less concerned with monotheism than the Protestant Christian missionaries who arrived in China in 1807. The Protestant missionaries in China were most concerned with spreading the belief that Christianity was the only true religion and its belief in a single, personal God.[11]

From reading numerous writings of British and American missionaries in the late nineteenth and early twentieth centuries, it is clear that monotheism in China was never an isolated issue, given the religious and historical context of both Christianity and China. From the Christian perspective, the discussion of monotheism could not be separated from that of polytheism and Christian cosmology. Although the foremost concern of Western missionaries was whether the religious system in ancient China was monotheistic or polytheistic, these missionaries were also concerned about whether it acknowledged the theory of creation, which was also a reference to whether it recognized the Creator as the only true God.

Moreover, during the interactions with their Chinese audience who were either educated literati or religious practitioners in the field, Western missionaries quickly realized that there were considerable differences between the ancient religious system they had learned about from old documents and the spiritual practices that they witnessed during their stay in China. When these missionaries arrived in China, Christianity was certainly not a dominant religion, and the Chinese practiced numerous forms of rituals and worship in their various cults. Therefore, these missionaries tried to find the historical roots of monotheism in ancient China as the basis for preaching the gospel. Gradually, they came to terms with the historical development of the religious systems in China, their continuity, and their constant changes, both textually and practically. They felt that if there were a continuous thread of monotheism woven throughout the Chinese religions, it might be easier for the Chinese to accept the Christian gospels. However, these missionaries argued that there had been a "degeneration" of Chinese religion from monotheism in ancient times to polytheism in more recent times.

Besides the religious and cultural background, European intellectual knowledge in the nineteenth and early twentieth centuries should also be taken into consideration. When these missionaries travelled to China to preach Christianity, many European explorers took advantage of colonial expansion in Asia to investigate ancient cultural remains. They recovered countless

---

[11] The Tract Committee, "Religion in China," in *Church Work in North China* (London: Society for Promoting Christian Knowledge, 1891), 108.

ancient manuscripts and artefacts from Asia. These new materials inspired European scholars to decipher some of the dead languages used in those ancient manuscripts and inscriptions, critically compile and edit them, and interpret the ancient religions of Asia to understand the cultural past of Europe as a modern civilization. For example, European explorers such as Aurel Stein (1862–1943) and Paul Pelliot (1878–1945) discovered numerous manuscripts in ancient and medieval Indo-Iranian languages from Central Asia that reshaped the contemporary understanding of Buddhism, Zoroastrianism, Manichaeism, and Nestorianism in Asia. The study of Indo-European philology and comparative religions benefited greatly from these discoveries of the Western colonial explorers in the nineteenth and early twentieth centuries.

Unavoidably, while discussing monotheism in the religious systems in ancient China, some British missionaries quickly learned about the process of discovering Asian antiquities and Europe's cultural heritage. They attempted to utilize some of the approaches of the flourishing study of philology in Europe to identify the vocabulary in ancient Chinese classics as philological evidence of monotheism. Many of them, such as Edkins, Soothill, James Legge, and Arthur C. Moule, devoted themselves to studying the traditional Chinese classics and eventually became Sinologists. They discussed key terms such as *Shangdi* (the Sovereign on High), *Di* (Thearch), *Tian* (Heaven), and *Taiji* (the Great Ultimate).[12] Some of them also realized that even the Confucian classics had a long history and they found that different texts from different historical eras had different vocabularies for the true God. Therefore, these debates also led to the so-called "term controversy" among the Christian missionaries – a controversy that has had a long history in Western missions to China. Long before the intellectual impact of Indo-European philology flourished in Europe, the Protestant Christian missionaries had inherited some similar debates and concepts from the Jesuits who had arrived in China two hundred years earlier than the Protestants. Therefore, there were multiple voices among these missionaries.

Moreover, the European missionaries also took note of and participated in the emergence of social sciences in modern Europe, such as the sociological and anthropological study of non-European religions and cultures. Since the Christian missionaries realized the difference between the philological study

---

[12] It should be noted that modern scholars in Chinese philosophy used different translations for these terms; for instance, H. H. Dubs used "the High-god" for *Di*, "the Supreme High-god" for *Shangdi*, and "Heaven" for *Tian*; see his article "Theism and Naturalism in Ancient Chinese Philosophy," *Philosophy East and West*, 9: 3–4 (1959), 166. Dubs argues that Confucius accepted "Heaven" as a single Supreme God and that his personal religious belief was high monotheism.

of Chinese religions and their own experience in the field,[13] they devoted themselves to studying the numerous cults and rituals practiced across the empire. They not only attempted to categorize the Chinese pantheon and make sense of these various rituals and cults but also examined the relationship of the cults to the more visibly institutionalized Three Teachings. The Protestant missionaries' preliminary investigations into these cults laid the foundation for the scientific study of Chinese religions in the twentieth century.[14]

2.2 The Jesuits: Forerunners in the Discussion of Monotheistic Terminology

First, let us look at the debates among the first generation of Jesuit missionaries in China. Interestingly, these Jesuits observed the popular ancestral cult among the Chinese and were concerned with the rites of offering sacrifices. However, they focused on their interactions with the well-educated Chinese literati and attempted to convert these dominant Chinese elite groups. To do this, the Jesuits studied the ancient Chinese texts, especially the Confucian classics. Their understanding of the Chinese religious world focused on what they had learned from the Confucian classics that were most widespread and popular of the classics among the Chinese literati.

In his monumental work, *The True Meaning of the Lord of Heaven* (Tianzhu shiyi), Matteo Ricci (1552–1610) attempted to attract well-educated Chinese scholar-officials by citing Confucian classical works and equating the Chinese Heaven (*Tian*) with the European Deus (*Zhu*).[15] As a Jesuit missionary, Ricci explained several vital concepts such as the existence of God, the immortality of the soul, and the divine judgment of good and evil. He developed a new strategy of cultural adaptation to convert the Chinese, reading European monotheism into various ancient Chinese texts, including the (Confucian) Four Books (namely the *Great Learning, The Doctrine of the Mean, The Analects*, and *Mencius*) as well as the Five Confucian Classics. Ricci had quickly encountered such critical terms as "*Tian* (Heaven)" and "*Shangdi* (the Sovereign on High)" and recognized them as higher powers. He read in the Confucian classical works

---

[13] Early European Sinologists already noted these two different approaches to China; see H. Cordier, *Half a Decade of Chinese Studies, 1886–1891* (Leiden: Brill, 1892).
[14] For instance, M. Granet, *La religion des Chinois* (Paris: Gauthier-Villars & Cie., 1922).
[15] Y. Liu, "Adapting Catholicism to Confucianism: Matteo Ricci's *Tianzhu Shiyi*," *The European Legacy*, 19: 1 (2014), 43–59; K. N. Cawley, "De-constructing the Name(s) of God: Matteo Ricci's Translational Apostolate," *Translation Studies*, 6: 3 (2013), 293–308; I. H. Chen, "From God's Chinese Names to a Cross-Cultural Universal God: James Legge's Intertextual Theology in His Translation of Tian, Di and Shangdi," *Translation Studies*, 9: 3 (2016), 268–281. T. Meynard "Chinese Buddhism and the Threat of Atheism in Seventeenth-Century Europe," *Buddhist-Christian Studies*, 31 (2011), 3–23.

that *Tian* as a supreme being was different from the physical heavens in the Chinese tradition, and he claimed that *Shangdi* and the (European) Lord of Heaven were different only in name. Although he claimed to have detected Chinese monotheism in the Confucian classical texts, he admitted that Confucianism in his era was radically different from Catholicism. He stated that the superior men worshipped the "Sovereign on High and the Lord of Heaven" and earth in ancient times. Still, according to Liu, Ricci said that he had heard of no one paying respect to the Supreme Ultimate (*Taiji*), the "originating propensity of the universe" in the Neo-Confucian cosmology. Ricci was also aware that this version of Confucian cosmology had been "corrupted" by Daoism and Buddhism.[16]

Ricci and his Chinese friend Qu Taisu (1549–1612) exchanged ideas about Catholicism and Confucianism. From Qu, when Ricci learned about the distinctions between early and late Confucianism, he became interested in seeking monotheism in the early tradition. Jacques Gernet suggests that Ricci's equation of the Confucian concept "*Tian*" with the European "Deus" created confusion among Chinese audiences and European missionaries.[17] He proposed a contrast between the anthropomorphic, personalized Christian God and the Chinese idea of an impersonal Heaven. Recently, however, Edward Slingerland has argued that "Heaven is less full-bloodedly anthropomorphic than, say, the Greek gods or Abrahamic God," but not entirely impersonal.[18]

Interestingly, Ricci called Confucianism, Buddhism, and Daoism sects of the literati, Shakyamuni, Laozi, and the literati, respectively, but he did not call Confucianism the sect of Confucius. However, he regarded all these "sects" as false religions that had gathered various false doctrines. Only Catholicism was the true religion for him.[19] Nevertheless, Ricci maintained that the Heaven worshipped by the Chinese of ancient times was not the Creator, and only the God of Catholicism was. Many Jesuit missionaries accepted and maintained this position. In his *The Learned Discussions at Sanshan* (Sanshan lunxue ji), Guilio Aleni also addressed the issues on the Great Ultimate in light of the Jesuit theology of the (Christian) Creation. According to Aleni, in Aristotelian natural philosophy, the Great Ultimate was the only material cause among the Four

---

[16] Y. Liu, "Adapting Catholicism to Confucianism," 47–48.
[17] J. Gernet, *China and the Christian Impact*, trans. by Janet Lloyd (Cambridge: Cambridge University Press, 1985), 71; J. Gernet, *Chine et Christianisme: Action et reaction* (Paris: Gallimard, 1982), 39–45.
[18] E. Slingerland, *Mind and Body in Early China: Beyond Orientalism and the Myth of Holism* (Oxford: Oxford University Press, 2019), 252; a more recent discussion also can be found in K. J. Clark and J. Winslett, *A Spiritual Geography of Early Chinese Thought* (London: Bloomsbury, 2023).
[19] T. H. Barrett, "Chinese Religion in English Guise: The History of an Illusion," *Modern Asian Studies*, 39: 3 (2005), 512.

Causes because it was the Prime Matter. This fundamental element formed the physical universe; therefore, the Great Ultimate could not be the same as the Creator. The Great Ultimate was not even close to the Lord of Heaven because it had a beginning and was not the root of all things.[20] Clearly, the Great Ultimate was emphasized by the Confucian literati in the seventeenth century, and it became the focus of some of the Jesuit concerns.

The concept of the Great Ultimate attracted the attention of these Jesuits because it had ontological meaning in Neo-Confucian thought in the Song and Ming Dynasties. However, when some of the missionaries later realized that this concept was not found in the ancient Confucian classics, it gradually faded from the debates on Confucian monotheism among the missionaries. As Chinese intellectual historian Chen Shouyi suggested, the Jesuit missionaries developed four viewpoints on Confucianism in late imperial China. First, Catholicism's Lord of Heaven was equated with the Sovereign on High in Confucian classical works rather than the Great Ultimate. Second, ancient Confucian scholars believed that the soul is immortal. Third, the Confucianism of the later periods was different from the original "pure" Confucianism. Fourth, the advanced thought of China was not wrong, but Catholicism was needed to supplement it.[21]

Contemporary scholars have also paid attention to the debates on the disputed terms. For example, Liam Brockley noted that the heated discussions over critical terms such as *Tian*, *Shangdi*, and *Tianzhu* and their implications for referring to the Christian God had divided the Jesuit missionaries in Macau when André Palmeiro arrived. These early missionaries indeed found these terms in the writings of Chinese antiquity exciting. For instance, in ancient Chinese writings, the character for *Tian* was often regarded as a reference to more than just the material heavens. However, there were disputes among the Jesuits on the Chinese concept of a Creator. While handling these debates, in August 1625, Superior General Muzio Vitelleschi even prohibited the use of the Chinese term "*Shangdi*" due to the vagueness of its meaning and asked Palmeiro to reevaluate these issues. Palmeiro held a conference in Jiading in 1627, and at that conference, almost all of the Jesuits agreed that the term "*Tian*" could not signify the Christian God and that the term "*Shangdi*" presented even more problems. Even the Chinese literati converts such as Yang Tingyun (1562–1627) and Li Zhizao (1565–1630) were confused about

---

[20] G. Song, *Giulio Aleni, Kouduo Richao, and Christian–Confucian Dialogism in Late Ming Fujian* (London: Routledge, 2018).

[21] S. Chen, "Mingmo Qingchu Yesuhuishi de rujiaoguan jiqi fanying [The Confucian View of Jesuit Missionaries and Their Responses in the Late Ming and Early Qing Periods]," in his *Zhong'ou wenhua jiaoliu shishi luncong* [Collected Papers on the History of the Cultural Exchanges between China and Europe] (Taipei: Shangwu yinshuguan, 1970), 13–18.

how these terms could truly refer to the Supreme Being in the Christian sense.[22] While working on the ancient Chinese texts with their Chinese converts, the Jesuits realized that Chinese civilization had existed long before the birth of Christ and could be compared with the accounts of Western society found in the Old Testament. They believed that the ancient Chinese documents used the terms *Tian* and *Shangdi* to refer to a deity who responded to human pleas. They attempted to identify the Chinese concepts with elements of the Christian revelation to demonstrate that the earliest Chinese knowledge about the Judeo-Christian God had come before the advent of Buddhism.[23] In other words, these Jesuits suggested that the Confucian canon contained implicit and explicit references to the Christian God.[24]

Later, in the seventeenth century, the Catholic missionaries, especially the Jesuits, Dominicans, and Franciscans, continued to debate the use of the Chinese rites. Although the Jesuits attempted to accommodate the needs of the Chinese Catholic followers by allowing them to carry out their traditional rites, the Dominicans and Franciscans disagreed. The latter reported the issue to the Roman Church and in 1704, Pope Clement XI intervened and forbade the use of the terms "*Tian*" and "*Shangdi*" as a translation of "God"; the Pope's decree instead insisted on the use of "*Tianzhu*" (Lord of the Heaven). In 1715, the Pope again condemned the carrying out of the Chinese rites and affirmed the use of "*Tianzhu*" for the Catholic word for God. These decrees aroused the ire of the Kangxi Emperor (1654–1722, r. 1661–1722), and in 1721, he banned the Catholic missionaries in China.[25] Kangxi's son the Yongzheng Emperor (1678–1735, r. 1722–1735) continued the policy of banning Christian missionary work, and he expelled the missionaries from China. The Jesuits, however, continued to secretly proselytize in the coastal cities of China.

The Catholic missionaries returned to China after the first Opium War (1840–1842) and most of them were sponsored by the French Société des Missions Etrangères de Paris.[26] Interestingly, besides the fact that the first

---

[22] L. M. Brockley, *Journey to the East: The Jesuit Mission to China, 1579–1724* (Cambridge, MA: Harvard University Press, 2007), 86–87; for the study on Yang Tingyun, see N. Standaert, *Yang Tingyun, Confucian and Christian in Late Ming China: His Life and Thought* (Leiden: Brill, 1988); J. Ji, *Encounters between Chinese Culture and Christianity: A Hermeneutical Perspective* (Berlin and Münster: LIT Verlag, 2007).

[23] Brockley, *Journey to the East*, 265.   [24] Brockley, *Journey to the East*, 284.

[25] D. E. Mungello, *The Chinese Rites Controversy: Its History and Meaning* (Nettetal: Steyler and Sankt Augustin: Institut Monumenta Serica, 1994).

[26] Many research works have focused on church-state relations or local Catholic communities in the latter half of the nineteenth century; see, for example, J. Heyndrickx ed., *Historiography of the Chinese Catholic Church: Nineteenth and Twentieth Centuries* (Leuven: Ferdinand Verbiest Foundation, K. U. Leuven, 1994); J. Kindopp and C. L. Hemrin eds., *God and Caesar in China: Policy Implications of Church-State Tensions* (Washington, DC: Brookings Institution Press, 2004); E. P. Young, *Ecclesiastical Colony: China's Catholic Church and the French Religious*

generation of Protestant missionaries benefited from the Jesuit missionaries in terms of their mission strategy and theological discussions, there were also interactions between the Catholic and Protestant communities along the coastal region of China.[27] The intellectual exchanges and mutual respect between Catholics and Protestant missionaries were manifested by publishing in missionary journals and newspapers and participating in meetings, especially in Shanghai. Yet in some remote areas, there were rivalries between Catholics and Protestant missionaries.[28] Nevertheless, as Henrietta Harrison has noted, in one local village in Shanxi, the Chinese Catholics worshiped the Lord of Heaven as the only Christian God and equated Jesus with Heaven, which was their own way of acknowledging Catholic monotheism. They also believed that there was only one teaching by this one God in the whole world and that only the pope in Rome spoke for this teaching.[29]

2.3 Protestant Missionaries on Chinese Monotheism

A similar strategy continued in the writings of the Protestant missionaries once they found themselves in China in the early nineteenth century. Before Robert Morrison arrived in China, William Winterbotham (1763–1829) might have been one of the earliest scholars from a Protestant background to discuss Chinese religions. He was originally a Baptist but he later converted to Calvinism. He never visited China, but he accessed some textual sources in England and developed his own ideas about Chinese religions. Some of the terms he used in his book, such as "state religion" and "ancient religion of China," later also appeared in many of the writings of Protestant missionaries.

Winterbotham first pointed out that it was necessary to distinguish "the ancient and permanent religion of the state" from "popular superstitions" in China. He noted that this so-called ancient and permanent religion was the only religion avowed by the government, followed by the emperor, grandees, and literati, and authorized to be publicly taught. He accepted the idea of Father Amiot about this ancient religion. For him,

---

Protectorate (Oxford: Oxford University Press, 2013); Ji Li, *God's Little Daughters: Catholic Women in Nineteenth-Century Manchuria* (Seattle: University of Washington Press, 2015).

[27] J. T. Lee analyzed the interactions between the French Catholic missionaries and American Baptist missionaries in northern Guangdong area; see *The Bible and the Gun: Christianity in South China, 1860–1900* (London and New York: Routledge, 2002), 119–136.

[28] S. Pieragastini, "Jesuit and Protestant Encounters in Jiangnan: Contest and Cooperation in China's Lower Yangzi Region," in J. Cañizares-Esguerra, R. A. Maryks, R. P. Hsia eds., *Encounters between Jesuits and Protestants in Asia and the Americas* (Leiden: Brill, 2018), 118.

[29] H. Harrison, *The Missionary's Curse and Other Tales from a Chinese Catholic Village* (Berkeley: University of California Press, 2013), 31, 61.

> The Canonical Books of the Chinese everywhere confirm the idea of a Supreme Being, the Creator and Preserver of all things. They mention him under the names of *Tian*, or Heaven; *Shangtian*, or Supreme Heaven; *Shangdi*, or Supreme Lord; and of *Huang shangdi*, or Sovereign and Supreme Lord; names corresponding to those which we use when we speak of divinity; God, the Lord, the Almighty, the Highest. "This Supreme Being," say these books, "is the principle of everything that exists, and the Father of all living; he is eternal, immovable, and independent; his power knows no bounds; his sight equally comprehends the past, the present, and the future, and penetrate even to the innermost recesses of the heart. Heaven and earth are under his government: all events, all revolutions are the consequences of his dispensations and will. He is pure, holy, and impartial; wickedness offends his sight, but he beholds with an eye of complacency the virtuous actions of men. Severe, yet just, he punishes vice in an exemplary manner, even in princes and rulers, and often precipitates the guilty, to crown with honor the man who walks after his own heart, and whom he hath raised from obscurity. Good, merciful, and full of pity, he forgives on the repentance of the wicked; and public calamities, and the irregularity of the seasons, are only helpful warnings, which his fatherly goodness give to men. To induce them to reform and amend."[30]

In this passage, Winterbotham indicates many qualities and virtues of the old Chinese concept of the Supreme Being and attempted to make it correspond to the Christian idea of God or Lord. For him, they were both omnipotent, mighty, and glorious. Winterbotham concludes by saying, "We see, in these monuments of remote antiquity, the most evident traces of the patriarchal faith; and that the ancient Chinese worshipped only one Supreme God, whom they considered as a free and intelligent Being, and as an all-powerful, avenging, and rewarding Spirit."[31] He emphasized that this concept had continued ever since, and through the ages, numerous Chinese rulers supported this religious doctrine of the first emperors of China, even up to his times. While he saw that multiple rebellions had shaken the royal thrones and overthrown the court powers, he noted that the Chinese constantly attributed all to the supreme direction of the Sovereign Lord of Heaven. This was the so-called Mandate of Heaven, though Winterbotham did not explicitly use this phrase. He also described various sacrifices offered by the emperors from ancient times up to the Qing Dynasty.

Interestingly, Winterbotham did not refer to this so-called ancient religion of China as Confucianism, and he never mentions Confucius or Confucianism in his discussion about this religion. In fact, Winterbotham's discussions on Chinese

---

[30] W. Winterbotham, *An Historical, Geographical, and Philosophical View of the Chinese Empire* (London: Printed for, and sold by J. Ridgway and W. Button, 1795), 320.

[31] Winterbotham, *An Historical, Geographical, and Philosophical View of the Chinese Empire*, 321.

religions did not even refer to Confucianism as a religion.³² Instead, Winterbotham referred to an ancient religion of China from the early times, which continued until his era, the Qing Dynasty. According to him, the followers of this ancient religion of China worshipped one omnipotent God who had absolute power to punish or reward the rulers and the ruled for their actions. The dynastic changes on the ground relied on the judgement and will of this all-powerful God. This ancient religion could also be regarded as the state religion since it was in charge of the ritual sacrifices. After the section on the old religion in China, he discussed Daoism and Buddhism and noted a degeneration from Daoist philosophy to the Daoist religion.³³

In 1807 Robert Morrison arrived in Macao as the first Protestant missionary in China. Ten years later, he published a book in Macao titled *A View of China for Philological Purpose Containing a Sketch of Chinese Chronology, Geography, Government, Religion and Customs*. It was written to introduce China and Chinese culture to English speakers. The section on religion discusses the three "sects" – Confucianism, Buddhism, and Daoism – along with Chinese popular religion.³⁴ His view on Chinese religions did not follow Winterbotham's suggestion to highlight a so-called "ancient religion of China," which might have been partially due to his experience in Macao, where he observed the religious practices of the local Chinese residents.

However, as his time in Macao grew longer, Morrison seemed to change his views on Chinese religions. He studied Chinese and read the Chinese texts, and he interacted with the local people. These intellectual and daily-life experiences must have dramatically contributed to his changing views of Chinese religions and China. In 1834, he published an essay to address the issue of state religion in China.³⁵ Morrison first pointed out that there was no generic term for religion in China. For him, the Chinese character for "*jiao*" meant to teach doctrine or to instruct, and it was used for all of the Three Teachings. By that time, he only referred to Daoism and Buddhism as religious sects, and he called Confucianism an ethical sect.³⁶

More importantly, Morrison separated the doctrinal teachings from the texts and the rites he observed in person. He developed the idea that the state religion

---

[32] In Britain, around that time, worldviews were commonly divided into deism and atheism. For example, see R. Adam, *The Religious World Displayed* (Edinburgh: Printed by James Ballantyne for Longman, Hurst, Rees, and Orme, 1808).

[33] Eventually, he briefly discussed Jews and Mahometans, but as a Christian, he did not emphasize on their monotheism.

[34] R. Morrison, *A View of China* (Macao: P. P. Thomas, 1817), 110–120.

[35] R. Morrison, "The State Religion of China," *Chinese Repository*, 3: 2 (June, 1834), 49–53.

[36] Some missionaries did not even use the words "religion" or "religions" when discussing the religious practices in China – they just used the terms "superstitions"; see, for example, S. Kidd, *China* (London: Taylor & Walton, 1841).

of China was a set of traditions and ceremonies without texts but based on the government code. He found no monotheism in this state religion. He noted that "*jiao*" should not apply to the state religion of China because this state religion did not consist of any doctrines that are taught, studied, and believed: it only consisted of rites and ceremonies, and it was entirely a bodily service. Morrison stated that the state religion was practiced by the court and provincial governments, following the Code of Laws of the Great Qing. He then offered a sketch of the rites of offering sacrifices and listed three classes of sacrifices and "gifts": great "gifts," medium sacrifices, and small sacrifices. In his observations, the entire material universe was worshiped in this state religion system. Various celestial and terrestrial gods were offered gifts or sacrifices. However, he did not mention the Upper Thearch (*Shangdi*), the highest god that appeared in Winterbotahm's writing.

Morrison also made a clear distinction between Confucianism and the state religion. He points out that although *rujiao* (the teachings of Confucian scholars), a philosophical rather than religious sect, monopolized both the civil and sacred functions in the government, the teachings of Confucius did not constitute the state religion. Confucianism was simply a set of doctrines and teachings, while the state religion was a set of rites and ceremonies based on governmental and legal codes.

However, while Morrison failed to identify the Supreme Being in the ancient Chinese religions, other Protestant missionaries never gave up on finding monotheism in China. In 1820, William Milne (1785–1822), who arrived in China slightly later than Morrison, argued that the earliest writings of the Chinese already contained "very clear and just sentiments concerning the Divine Being" but that they did not continue in the later writings of the Chinese. He believed that the Five Classics of Confucianism, especially the *Book of Documents* (Shujing), were produced by writers who lived in the "primitive" ages of Chinese history. In these works, "the light of traditional revelation was less obscured by idolatry and superstition."[37] For him, the worship of the heavens and the earth was the most ancient kind of Chinese idolatry; and, though the Chinese beliefs had probably never been free of idolatry, Daoism and Buddhism significantly increased it through their introduction of various gods and deities into the lives of Chinese people. Thus, Milne sought monotheism in the most ancient documents in the Confucian classics and he raised the issue of idolatry "pollution" in Daoism and Buddhism.[38]

---

[37] W. Milne, *A Retrospect of the First Ten Years of the Protestant Mission to China* (Malacca: The Anglo-Chinese Press, 1820), 25–27.

[38] For the missionary writings on Chinese Buddhism, see J. Edkins, *Chinese Buddhism* (London: Kegan Paul, Trench, and Trübner, 1880); E. J. Eitel, *Handbook for the Student of Chinese Buddhism* (London: Trübner, 1870); E. J. Eitel, *Three Lectures on Buddhism* (Hong Kong: At the London Mission House, and London: Trübner, 1871). Both Milne and Legge noticed the work of the Jesuits and they attempted to distinguish Protestant Christianity from Catholicism to their

The number of Protestant missionaries arriving in China increased and so did the number of translations of Christian texts into Chinese for the purpose of proselytization. In the process of the translation enterprise, accurately summarizing the critical terms from Christianity became a pressing issue. Following in the steps of the Jesuit missionaries in China in the seventeenth century, the Protestant missionaries gradually joined the conversations and debates on the terms used for translating God and other key concepts, as they were concerned about how to precisely render the concept of Christian monotheism and make it accessible to the Chinese. For example, English Congregationalist missionary Walter Henry Medhurst (1796–1857) and London Mission Society missionary John Stronach (1810–1888) suggested translating "God" into the Chinese word "*Shangdi*." For Merdhurst, in ancient Chinese texts, "*Shangdi*" was the same as "*Tian*," and "god" could be used to refer to various spirits. He also pointed out that the Chinese word "*tianming* (the Mandate of Heaven)" indeed reflected the will of Heaven or *Shangdi*.[39] The first American Protestant missionary to China, Elijah Coleman Bridgman (1801–1861), and the American Episcopalian missionary William Jones Boone (1811–1864) argued against using the word "*shen*" as a translation for "God." Boone noted that the Chinese were polytheistic and did not understand the true God, so they must accept a commonly known word for the highest True God among numerous gods and deities. American Presbyterian missionary Walter Macon Lowrie (1819–1847) had a similar concern with Chinese polytheism.

These missionaries were not professional Sinologists nor had they read much in the ancient Chinese classics. In contrast to Merdhurst's suggestion based on his observations of widespread religious practices in China, one of the most learned British missionaries, James Legge (1815–1897), joined the discussion with a strong background in the study of the ancient Chinese texts. He cited old Chinese classics and the Great Ming Code to point out that there was a monotheistic faith in China in ancient times, and "*Shangdi*" in the minds of the Chinese was the same as "God" in Christianity. He even claimed that the Chinese in the bygone era had the concept of a creator.[40]

Chinese audience, though the Jesuits indeed had an impact on their missionary work in terms of adapting vernacular Chinese; see S. L. Wei, "Jesuits' and Protestants' Use of Vernacular Chinese in Their Accommodation Policy," in J. Cañizares-Esguerra, R. A. Maryks, and R. P. Hsia eds., *Encounters between Jesuits and Protestants in Asia and the Americas* (Leiden: Brill, 2018), 73–89.

[39] S. Johnson accepted his ideas, see his *Oriental Religions and their Relations to Universal Religion: China*, part II (Boston: Houghton, Mifflin, 1877), 723–733, on "theism."

[40] J. Legge, *An Argument for Shang-te As the Proper Rendering of the Words Elohim and Theos, In the Chinese Language* (Hong Kong: Printed at the Register Office, 1850); J. Legge, *The Notions of the Chinese Concerning God and Spirits* (Hong Kong: Printed at the Register Office, 1852); for the discussion on Legge, see L. F. Pfister, *Striving for "The Whole Duty of Man"* (Frankfurt and Main: Peter Lang, 2004); N. J. Girardot, *The Victorian Translation of China: James Legge's Oriental Pilgrimage* (Berkeley: University of California Press, 2002), 43–44, 86–89, 221–223.

But the heated debate on this crucial term continued. When the Protestant missionaries organized a New Testament Translation Committee of the Delegates' version of the Chinese Bible Translation (CBT), they began to discuss how to translate the name of God into Chinese.[41] They first debated the so-called "Term Question" during a conference in Hong Kong in 1843. In the 1840s and 1850s, the *Chinese Repository* published articles discussing various possible translations of this key term. By 1860, the American churches in China used "God," while the English missionaries, especially those from the London Mission Society, preferred *"Shangdi."* However, some English missionaries accepted the use of "God." Later, a new wave of debates over the translations of God appeared in the *Chinese Recorder* in the 1870s. Subsequently, the Protestant missionaries raised the same issue at conferences in 1877, 1890, and 1907 in Shanghai.

During the First General Missionary conference in Shanghai in 1877, on May 22, J. S. Roberts presented an essay titled "Principles of Translation into Chinese," which briefly touched upon the issue on how to translate the Chinese character *"shen."* He noted that there were two analogues in English and in the original tongues of the Scriptures. One was *"spirit, pneuma,* or *ruach,"* and the other referred to "gods" – *"elohim,"* and *"theos."*[42] James Legge's paper "Confucianism in Relation to Christianity" quickly generated debates among the missionaries. However, eventually the participants of this conference decided to omit referring to the Term Question in the published record, so

---

J. Chalmers, "Chinese Natural Theology," in V. De Rosen ed. *Travaux de la Troisième session du Congrès International des Orientalistes, St Pétersbourg, 1876*. Tome deuxième (Leiden: E. J. Brill, 1879), 15–39; G. Owen (1843–1914), *The Chinese Recorder and Missionary Journal* 18 (Shanghai: American Presbyterian Mission Press, August, 1886), 285–293; (September, 1886), 329–337.

[41] For a concise introduction to the Bible translation and its relation to the debate on term question, see L. Pfister, "Bible Translations and the Protestant 'Term Question,'" in R. G. Tiedemann ed., *Christianity in China, vol. 2, 1800-present* (Leiden: Brill, 2010), 361–370; J. O. Zetzsche, *The Bible in China: The History of the Union Version or the Culmination of Protestant Missionary Bible Translation in China* (Sankt Augustin: Monumenta Serica Insitut, 1999), 82–90.

[42] The Editorial Committee, *Records of the General Conference of the Protestant Missionaries of China held at Shanghai, May 10–24, 1877* (Shanghai: Presbyterian Mission Press, 1878), 418–426, esp. 420. Several missionaries joined the discussion but did not pay much attention to the term question. In the conference held in 1890, no particular paper addressed the term question, though on May 7, William Muirhead briefly noted the history of translating word "God" into Chinese, tracing it back to the Nestorian church and also to the Jesuits' debates on using *"Tianzhu"* or *"Shen."* See his essay "Historical Summary of the Different Versions. With Their Terminology, and the Feasibility of Securing a Single Standard Version in Wen-li, with a Corresponding Version in Mandarin Colloquial," in the Editorial Committee ed., *Records of the General Conference of the Protestant Missionaries of China held at Shanghai, May 7–20, 1890* (Shanghai: American Presbyterian Mission Press, 1890), 33–41. Subsequently, several other missionaries also discussed the versions in their essays, without focusing on the term question.

Legge's paper did not appear in the conference proceedings.[43] Interestingly, even though Legge was a well-respected scholar among many missionaries, his views on the term "*Shangdi*" in Chinese religions were not accepted by the *Chinese Repository*.[44] The centenary conference of missionaries in Shanghai in 1907 did not focus on the "Term Question" either, although there was a session devoted to ancestral worship.[45]

Legge's legacy continued in the writings of some other missionaries. For instance, James Dyer Ball gave a series of lectures on the religions of the Chinese at the Young Men's Christian Association (YMCA) in Hong Kong in 1905. He published these lectures as a collected volume titled *The Celestial and His Religions: The Religious Aspect in China* in 1906. The first lecture focused on the primeval conception of God in China and the "primitive" religion of the Chinese.[46]

---

[43] I. Eber, "The Interminable Term Question," in I. Eber, S. Wan, K. Walf, and R. Malek eds., *Bible in Modern China: The Literary and Intellectual Impact* (Sankt Angustin: Institut Monumenta Serica, Nettetal: Steyler Verlag, 1999), 157–158.

[44] S. W. Williams, "The Controversy among the Protestant Missionaries on the Proper Translation of the Words God and Spirit into the Chinese," *Bibliotheca Sacra*, 35 (October, 1878), 739; W. J. Boone, *An Essay on the Proper Rendering of the Words Elohim and Theos into the Chinese Language* (Canton: Printed at the Office of the Chinese Repository, 1848), v; S. C. Malan, *Who Is God in China, Shin or Shang-Te? Remarks on the Etymology of Theos and Elohim and on the Rendering of Those Terms into Chinese* (London: Samuel Bagster, 1855), 33, 38, 286–287; *Jubilee Papers of the Central China Presbyterian Mission. 1844–1894. comprising historical sketches of the mission stations at Ningpo, Shanghai, Hangchow, Soochow, and Nanking, with a sketch of the Presbyterian Mission Press* (Shanghai: Printed at the American Presbyterian Mission Press, 1895), 36–37. G. Lillegard, *The Chinese Term Question: An Analysis of the Problem and Historical Sketch of the Controversy* (Boston: Christian Book Room, 1929); D. G. Spelman, "Christianity in Chinese: The Protestant Term Question," *Papers on China*, 22A (East Asian Research Center, Harvard University, May, 1969), 25–52; I. Eber, "The Interminable Term Question," in Irene Eber, Sze-kar Wan, and Knut Walf in collaboration with Roman Malek eds., *Bible in Modern China: The Literary and Intellectual Impact*. Monumenta Serica Monograph series XLIII. (Sankt Augustin: Institut Monumenta Serica, in cooperation with the Harry S. Truman Research Institute for the Advancement of Peace, The Hebrew University of Jerusalem. Nettetal: Steyler Verlag, 1999), 135–161; D. S. Ahn, "The Term Question in China: The Theological Factors behind the Translation of Shangti as the Term for 'God' in the Chinese Bible in the Nineteenth Century," in P. 'Iolana and S. Tongue eds., *Self, Faith, Interpretation and Changing Trends in Religious Studies* (New Castle upon Tyne: Cambridge Scholars Publishing, 2011), 95–114; Ahn noted that Legge was well aware of the Chinese rites controversy between the Jesuits, Dominicans, and Franciscans. Legge asserted that Pope Clement XI did not clearly apprehend the true meaning of *Shangdi*, so the Pope's decree favored the use of the "Lord of Heaven" rather than God.

[45] The Conference Committee, *China Centenary Missionary Conference Records. Report of the Great Conference held at Shanghai, April 5th to May 8th, 1907* (New York: American Tract Society, Printed in Shanghai, 1907). For a brief note on this conference, see K. X. Yao, "At the Turn of Century: A Study of the China Centenary Missionary Conference of 1907," *International Bulletin of Missionary Research*, 32: 2 (2008), 65–70.

[46] It was a common perception that the so-called primitive religions were different from other institutionalized religions in China; for example, G. T. Bettany, *Primitive Religions, Being an Introduction to the Study of Religions, with an Account of the Religious Beliefs of Uncivilised Peoples, Confucianism, Taoism (China), and Shintoism (Japan)* (London: Ward, Lock, and Bowden, 1891).

Ball admitted that he learned about the primitive conception of God among the Chinese and the early beliefs and superstitions in China from some knowledgeable Sinologists, especially James Legge. Thus, he noted that the character *Tian* (Heaven) and the term *Shangdi* (the Supreme Ruler) were interchangeable terms in the Chinese Classics. He suggested this tended towards the side of monotheism. He concluded that the early Chinese had mixed ideas about their beliefs.

On the one hand, monotheism appeared in their belief in one Supreme Ruler. On the other hand, polytheism also appeared because below this Supreme Ruler were a host of lesser spirits that were also worshipped.[47] Ball compared the worship of trees, animals, and stones with Western Asian traditions, such as Persian religions and the ancient religion of Israel. Therefore, he argued that

> in the earliest days of Chinese life there would appear to have been a monotheistic conception of a Supreme Being, but, as time went on, it was supplemented, or blended, with a polytheistic idea of a Valhalla of heroes and a pantheon of subordinate deities, while the rankist superstition attained a tropical growth; and hence the original and purer notions of a more exalted god above all had its development, if any, retarded there was a degeneracy – the conception has been atrophied.[48]

Ball hoped the missionaries could lead the Chinese to their original belief in One Supreme Being, God overall.

Since the nineteenth century, other Protestant missionaries had inherited some of Winterbotham's ideas on Chinese religions. They believed that the Chinese people in ancient times were less superstitious and had accepted (Christian) monotheism. For example, John Macgowan (1835–1922), a missionary in Amoy from the London Mission Society, commented about the religious systems on Chinese history:

> There are two great facts in Chinese history which are exceedingly striking, and the very existence of which places that nation on a higher platform than has ever been occupied by any heathen people. The first is, there has never been any deification of vice in China ... [and] the following fact is, as far as history informs us, there is no record of human sacrifices being offered up to appease offended deities for at least twenty-five centuries and not the slightest indication from the early

---

[47] J. D. Ball, *The Celestial and His Religions: The Religious Aspect in China*, a series of lectures on the religions of the Chinese (Hong Kong: Messes, Kelly and Walsh, 1906), 9.
[48] Ball, *The Celestial and His Religions*, 26.

writings that such a practice was known in ancient times. In this respect, the Chinese stand infinitely higher than any other heathen nation of which we have the record.[49]

So Macgowan, coming to China for the first time, understood the Chinese as a very religious people. He went on to point out that in ancient times, the people of China recognized the existence of a great Supreme Ruler who was aware of men's affairs and who punished vice and rewarded virtue.[50]

From his belief in his discovery of Chinese "monotheism" in ancient times, Macgowan turned to discuss the deterioration of this old belief in monotheism over time. He claimed that the Chinese views of God gradually became thoroughly materialized because the Chinese lost "the conception of a purely spiritual and independent Being, who is everywhere present, and whose will and commands should be the guide and rule of life."[51] He also noted that this deterioration of the old belief in monotheism eventually led to various beliefs being held in under Confucianism, Buddhism, and Daoism. However, he also claimed that, though the ordinary people engaged in different types of religious ceremonies, the emperor and the officers employed by the government throughout the empire practiced a state religion in which they offered three classes of state sacrifices. The first class included those to Heaven, earth, the imperial ancestors, and the gods of the land and grain. The second class were those made to the sun and moon, the spirits of former emperors, Confucius, and the gods of agriculture, silk, the passing year, and the gods of Heaven and earth. The third class included those presented to the spirits of deceased philanthropists, honest politicians, eminent scholars, the North Pole, clouds, rain, thunder, mountains, the Four Seas, and all the other waters and oceans. Thus, in his understanding, even though Confucianism was not the Chinese state religion, the state religion included a sacrificial rite to Confucius.

It should be noted that "state religion" in the Western sense was different from that of China as it was defined in the writings of the Western missionaries. In England, there was the Church of England that appointed bishops to lead local branch churches in constructing a national network of the churches. However,

---

[49] D. Matheson, *Narrative of the Mission to China of the English Presbyterian* Church, with remarks on the social life and religious ideas of the Chinese by the Rev. John Macgowan, and notes on climate, health, and outfit, by John Carnegie (London: James Nisbet, 1866), 119–120.

[50] The political implications of this Supreme Ruler are clearly manifested in the writing of E. H. Parker: "In the year B.C. 2356 the Supreme Ruler had decided not to pass on the imperial authority to a worthless son, but to confer it upon a worthy Minister, who had assisted in bringing about many of the above extensions or reforms. ... One of the new ruler's first acts was to appoint an officer of worship, charged with ritual duties towards the spirits of heaven and earth, and towards the manes [cb: Is "manes" correct?] of individuals." See his *China and Religion* (New York: E. P. Dutton, 1905), 22–23.

[51] D. Matheson, *Narrative of the Mission to China of the English Presbyterian Church*, 121.

under the Chinese so-called state religion, no national church appointed its local leaders. The court as the political authority oversaw the local sacrificial rites. Performing the rites such as offering sacrifices to Heaven, earth, and the Confucian temple was part of the work of local administrators. Unlike the priests in the Church of England, those in the local temples in China did not belong to a national-wide network. The Chinese governments in the imperial dynasties often specified the roles and functions of the different sets of sacrificial rites in their legal codes and canonized some popular sacrificial rites in local regions. However, usually the administration of the royal family's sacrificial rites remained within the court under the institutional system responsible for the family affairs of the emperor; in contrast, the sacrificial rites of the state were usually administered by the Department of Rites within the executive branch of the court. In China, no national church within the central government served as the head of the churches across the empire. Under Confucianism, for example, the temple for worshiping Confucius in the capital city never functioned as the head of all Confucian temples across the empire.

3 Monotheism and Polytheism: From Ancient Religion to State Religion

3.1 Introduction

Seeking monotheism in the Chinese religions led the Protestant missionaries to read the Chinese classics which led to the recognition that Confucianism was the state ideology. While some ministers were still concerned about the existence of monotheism in the ancient religious systems of China, others examined the relationship between monotheism in the ancient religions of China and the state religion of the Chinese empire. They debated whether the state ideology of the Chinese empire was a religion and whether this religious form preserved the monotheistic concepts found in the earliest religious systems of ancient China. As I have documented in the previous section, some missionaries quickly acknowledged Confucianism's status as the state religion, and, however, that there was no traditional Chinese concept of state religion. Whether the state ideology of the Chinese empire could be identified as the state religion depended on the historical context. The modern idea of a state religion was introduced into China by the Anglo-Saxonian missionaries. To convert the Chinese ruling class, the Western missionaries felt it important to examine monotheism in the dominant traditions of the Three Teachings, especially Confucianism, the state ideology.

When the first British Protestant missionaries came to China in 1807, most of them seemed to have accepted the concept of the nation-state in Europe and the concept of the state religion in Britain. For example, in England, Anglicanism was institutionalized as the state religion. When the British missionaries reached China and tried to understand China and Chinese religions, it made sense for them to try to understand them from a nation-state framework. They tried to determine if the Chinese state had a national religion[52] and a state religion, either in ancient or contemporary periods.

3.2 Monotheism in the State Religion of China

Some Protestant missionaries proposed that Confucianism was the state religion of China and developed their discussions of monotheism in China based on their understanding of Confucianism as such. For example, in his 1859 book titled *The Chinese Mission*, William Dean (1807–1895), the first Baptist missionary to China, understood Chinese religions in the historical framework of Christianity. He suggested that Chinese history could be traced back to the immediate descendants of Noah and that the early Chinese fathers retained some correct ideas of the true God. Later, Chinese polytheism replaced this monotheism, and with it came numerous images and objects for worshipping the gods of the heavens, earth, sun, moon, stars, rain, winds, seasons, and many others. Then he claimed that the votaries of these multiple forms of idolatry could be divided into three classes: Confucianism, Buddhism, and Daoism. After some brief reflections on the life of Confucius and his philosophy, Dean, whose views on Confucianism differed from those of Winterbotham and Morrison, concluded that "Confucianism, in short, a system of the theism, is the state religion of China. Its disciples, however, incorporate in their practices many of the ceremonies of other religious creeds."[53] He viewed Confucianism as the state religion and a type of theism, not just a sect of philosophers. However, he also claimed that Confucius himself was an atheist who had ignored the idea of an immortal soul. Confucianism was theism, but Confucius was an atheist philosopher, and according to Dean, Confucius's disciples transformed Confucianism from atheism to theism by introducing numerous rites and ceremonies.

Due to the powerful influence of Confucianism as a state ideology in the Chinese empire, some missionaries attempted to identify the monotheistic element in this tradition. William Muirhead was developed perhaps the most comprehensive interpretation of monotheism in Confucianism. In 1879 in Japan, he published a catechism on the five teachings of China, not in English

---

[52] In the European discourse at that time, the concept of national religion was different from that of universal religion; see A. Kuenen, *National Religions and Universal Religions*, Hibbert Lectures in 1882, translated by P. H. Wicksteed (London: Macmillan, 1882).
[53] W. Dean, *The Chinese Mission* (New York: Sheldon, 1859), 57–59.

but in Chinese. Muirhead was born in Leith in 1822 and became a minister in 1846; not long after, he was sent to Shanghai as a missionary by the London Mission Society. In 1861, he witnessed the Heavenly Kingdom of Great Peace movement (also known as the Taiping Rebellion) during a one-month stay in Nanjing. However, as a missionary leader mostly based in Shanghai, he translated the Bible into Chinese and focused on charitable activities in the neighboring regions. He passed away in Shanghai on October 3, 1900. As someone who had spent more than half a century in China, he was one of the most knowledgeable missionaries on the topics of Chinese religions and Chinese culture, and China in general, from his tremendous daily experience.

In the catechism titled *A General Introduction to the Five Teachings* (Wujiao tongkao), Muirhead claimed that only Christianity was the true and correct religion, and the four other teachings in China (Confucianism, Buddhism, Daoism, and Islam) were false religions.[54] He offered a brief introduction to Confucianism, which echoed some of the ideas of several of his contemporary missionaries. In particular, he mentioned that Confucianism had developed a set of sacrificial rites in which there was the concept of *Shangdi* (the Sovereign on High). At the beginning of his catechism, Muirhead said Confucianism had taught ancient kings and sages in China. According to him, these ancient kings and sages included Yao, Shun, Yu, Tang, King Wen, King Wu, Duke Zhou, and Confucius. The core of Confucian morality was the Three Fundamental Bonds (*sangang*) and Five Constant Virtues (*wuchang*).

Muirhead also paid particular attention to the rites of Confucianism that followed a set of rules and protocols for making sacrificial offerings to *Shangdi*, various gods and deities, and the ancestors. According to his interpretation, *Shangdi* actually existed, and he was also known as *Tian* and *Shangtian* (Upper Heaven on High)," or *Huangtian* (the Heaven of the August); Heaven was the physical form of *Shangdi* who gave birth to the myriad things. Muirhead found that this idea was close to the concept of the creator in Christianity. He noted that Confucianism taught the Chinese people to respect the Sovereign on High, to fear Heaven, and to serve Heaven. He also wrote that the rulers must offer sacrifices to Heaven to show their gratitude for its blessings and ordinary people must also offer sacrifices to Heaven to bless the supplies of food and clothes.

---

[54] Many other books also offer a survey of the five religions in China, such as Parker's *China and Religion*; and S. W. Williams 's *The Middle Kingdom: A Survey of the Geography, Government, Literature, Social Life, Arts and History of the Chinese Empire and Its Inhabitants* (London: Kegal Paul, 1883). In his book *Tianzhu shiyi*, Matteo Ricci claimed that only Catholicism was true. For the discussion on this issue, see J. Gernet, *Chine et Christianisme: Action et reaction* (Paris: Gallimard, 1982), 31–33.

Interestingly, Muirhead criticized Zhu Xi (1130–1200) for claiming that Heaven was the principle (*Li*) and the Great Ultimate (*Taiji*) by arguing that Zhu Xi failed to realize that Heaven was "*Zhuzai* (the Supreme Master)" who ruled over all spirits and humans and the myriad things he created.[55] For Muirhead, the Sovereign on High or Heaven was omnipotent, and this absolute power created the perfect order among all things between heaven and earth. This interpretation specified the monotheistic concept in Confucianism, distinguishing it from the Neo-Confucianism developed by Zhu Xi. It indicated that later Confucian thinkers such as Zhu Xi had caused the original monotheistic concept to degenerate. Nevertheless, this was an acculturation interpretation that served Christian purposes.

Although Muirhead claimed that he had already identified God as the creator and Supreme Master in Confucianism, he realized that Confucianism was a polytheistic because it developed a large pantheon of gods and deities of heaven, earth, mountains and rivers, and as well as soil and grain. He suggested that the rulers sacrificed to these gods and deities to receive blessings and expel evil. However, he pointed out that the authority of these gods and deities belonged to Heaven. He urged the Chinese people to abandon them and submit to God's true and eternal authority. In other words, he aimed to replace Chinese polytheism under Confucianism with Christian monotheism. He specifically raised harsh criticisms against ancestral worship in China. For him, the Chinese worshipped the ancestors due to their profound fear of them. He also criticized the worship of and sacrifices to the worthies, such as the martial gods Yue Fei and Duke Guan, who received had honorary titles from the central court early in Chinese history. Muirhead regarded this worship as idolatry that betrayed rationality and the ancient tradition of worshipping Heaven.

As a London Mission Society missionary, Muirhead eagerly proclaimed that Christianity was the only true religion in the world. He cited the Bible and claimed that eventually, all nations would convert to Christianity. Muirhead pointed out that the Three Teachings in China were the ways of humans. Christianity was the way of Heaven, since the Way of Heaven could expel delusions and enlighten people, gradually get rid of strange customs, revive transparent and clear politics, and help the people behave on their own, eventually bringing peace to all "under Heaven." Some of the wordings in Muirhead's writing seem to adapt the typical expression of the Confucian political and social ideal, indicating that Muirhead aimed at confronting and challenging

---

[55] For the study of Zhu Xi's discourses in the history of Confucianism, see H. C. Tillman, *Confucian Discourse and Chu Hsi's Ascendancy* (Honolulu: University of Hawai'i Press, 1992).

Confucianism as the dominant state ideology when he was in China. He pointed out that Christianity could help China diminish the popularity of idolatry in the Three Teachings because those teachings did not cover the idea of *Shangdi* and the soul's immortality. For Muirhead, Christianity was superior to the Three Teachings because Jesus Christ taught people to manifest the magnificent blessings of God and save everyone.[56] Muirhead was one of the few missionaries who touched upon all the crucial issues in Confucianism, such as God, creation, and immortality, from a Christian perspective.

Following the lead of Muirhead, Arthur Evans Moule (1836–1918) also suggested that Confucianism preserved the ancient faith in the one true God, though in a clouded form, because it condemned gross idolatry, commanded respect, and carried conviction through its high standards of morality, drawing down the love and reverence of the people from God to man. However, he realized that the reverence for Confucius, parents, and ancestors was a religion.[57] In his eyes, in contrast to Confucianism, Buddhism was atheistic because God and gods were all placed in a position subordinate to the Buddha. He regarded Daoism as an abject imitation of Buddhism. Laozi's god was Nature. Some centuries after the death of Laozi, his followers deified him and called him a *Shangdi*, associating with him two other deities, the triad of *Shangdi*, or the Three Pure Ones.[58]

Some Western missionaries even claimed that monotheism existed in both Confucianism and Daoism. For instance, Jas Johnston, a missionary from the Presbyterian Church of England, published a book in 1897 titled *China and Formosa* and devoted one chapter to discussing the practical religion of the Chinese. He believed that the three Chinese religions' original and historical forms were free from idolatrous rites and teaching. He even suggested that Confucianism and Daoism taught the unity and fatherhood of God in ancient times when they were "purer." However, Buddhism was different because even though its original form was free from idolatry, it seemed to deny the existence of a God. Johnston concluded that the worship of ancestors stood between the soul

---

[56] Muirhead, *Wujiao tongkao*, 52–53.
[57] For the study of the cult of Confucius, see J. X. Huang, *Youru shengyu: Quanli, Xinyang yu zhengdangxing* [Ascending the Holy Realm: Power, Belief, and Legitimacy] (Taipei: Yuncheng wenhua chuban gongsi, 1994); J. X. Huang, *Shengxian yu shengtu: lishi yu zongjiao lunwenji* [Sages and Saints: Collected Papers on History and Religions] (Taipei: Yuncheng wenhua chuban gongsi, 2001); T. A. Wilson, "Culture, Society, Politics, and the Cult of Confucius," in T. A. Wilson, ed., *On Sacred Grounds: Culture, Society, Politics, and the Formation of the Cult of Confucius* (Cambridge, MA: Center for Asian Studies, Harvard University, 2002), 1–40; T. A. Wilson, "Sacrifice and the Imperial Cult of Confucius," *History of Religions*, 41: 3 (2002), 251–287; T. A. Wilson, "The Ritual Formation of Confucian Orthodoxy and the Descendants of the Sage," *The Journal of Asian Studies*, 55: 3 (1996), 559–584.
[58] A. E. Moule, *Four Hundred Million: Chapters on China and the Chinese* (London: Seeley, Jackson, & Halliday, 1871), 30–33.

and God and became the greatest obstacle to the progress of Christianity. "It is the only real religious obstacle in the way of the spread of the Gospel, and almost the only excuse for intolerance and persecution on religious grounds."[59] He regarded the Confucian ethics for dealing with the Five [family and societal] Bonds as popular Confucianism, a system of political morality, rather than a religion. In a similar sense, he saw Daoism as a gross, vulgar system of divination, enchantment, and demon worship to the great masses of Chinese people. Therefore, he recognized that old forms of Confucianism and Daoism did preserve a concept of God, but Buddhism did not.

It should be noted that many Protestant missionaries in the nineteenth century regarded Confucianism as a set of political and moral systems rather than as a religion in the Western sense. For example, A. H. Smith (1845–1932) viewed Confucianism as a set of political and moral principles and partially as a state religion of China. Based on his reading of the classical Confucian texts, he suggested that Confucius was not interested in defining the relations between humans and God and was only interested in developing a set of moral principles to serve politics and society. Therefore, Confucius's teaching was not a religion because religion dealt with humans and God in the Western sense. However, he maintained that, though Confucius himself might not be religious, he was not against religion.[60] Indeed, in the West, viewing classical Confucianism as humanism rather than theism has a long history.

3.3 Monotheism in the Chinese Religions from the Perspective of European Philology

The missionaries mentioned above were by no means professionally trained Sinologists. However, some of them, such as Joseph Edkins, James Legge, and William Edward Soothill, were much stronger academically and were eventually were recognized as scholars by the non-religious academic institutions. They became the founding scholars in the modern study of Chinese religions. Joseph Edkins, for example, was one of the most significant of the missionaries-turned Sinologists. He published a book discussing beliefs in China.[61] Like Muirhead, he almost touched upon every crucial issue on monotheism in Chinese religions, such as God, a creator, and immortality. He seemed to have read numerous philosophical writings in both the classical and Song Confucian traditions. He claimed that although Confucius stated the Great Extreme (*Taiji*) was at the beginning of all things, he remained silent about what exactly it was.

---

[59] J. Johnston, *China and Formosa* (London: Harzell, Watson, & Viney, 1897), 48–53, esp. 53.
[60] A. H. Smith, *The Uplift of China* (New York: Young People's Missionary Movement, 1907), 88–98.
[61] J. Edkins, *Religion in China* (London: Kegan Paul, Trench, Trübner, 1893).

Edkins also discussed how other Confucian thinkers understood the Great Extreme. He found that in the writings of these thinkers, it was identical with the ultimate reason (*Daoli*) and even with God (*Shangdi*), though in Confucianism, creation was a spontaneous process, and not carried out by any single agent; and God had no personality. Edkins also believed that there was faith in the character of God in the old Chinese system, but that this faith was lost in the later Confucian tradition. Here, Edkins clearly distinguished the ancient and modern Confucian systems. He was inclined to believe that the authentic religion of the Chinese was monotheistic because it had a concept of God – the Supreme Ruler who was infinitely just, reasonable, and mighty. Edkins found that Buddhism had greatly influenced the original Chinese beliefs, even though the latter mixed its rites with the worship of ancestors. The ancestral cult became the most important among all the rites and ceremonies in China.[62]

Edkins argued that the ancient Chinese were undoubtedly more religious than the modern for insofar as they frequently mentioned God under the name of *Shangdi*. He claimed that the earliest books of China indeed provided evidence for this. However, though the ancient Chinese did hold the concept of God, it was not the same as Christianity because the Chinese offered sacrifices to other spirits besides God. He thought that the Chinese perhaps regarded these spirits as the angels in the Bible. He said, "The Chinese very early had the conception of powerful beings, subordinate to God, regulating the course of events in the physical and intellectual universe. They called them "*Shen* (God)." Edkins continued to notice inconsistencies in the views held by the Chinese in regard to the duty of worshipping God. Some felt that "Heaven should be worshipped only by the emperor in the name of the nation, and the God of Heaven is too majestic and glorious for a common person to dare approach Him as a worshipper."[63] In other words, the educated literati class had different views on God and the sacrificial rites from the ordinary people in China. Many familiar people did not differentiate between Heaven and God because they were not accustomed to the conception of a purely immaterial being; instead, they held the notions of God as a materialized form.

More specifically, Edkins discussed the details of ancient Chinese monotheism. First, the ancient Chinese believed in God as a personal, active being, the ruler of heaven and earth who was just, powerful, and merciful. However, this belief as explicit knowledge of God gradually faded among the descendants through the ages. According to Edkins, "If the attributes of God, according to

---

[62] J. Edkins, *Religion in China*, 71–75. [63] J. Edkins, *Religion in China*, 91–92.

the common notions of the Chinese were examined, they would prove a most manifest need of the light of revelation." He firmly believed that:

> We find that the Confucian religion is monotheistic, recognizing one Supreme Ruler, the tradition of whom the Chinese had from the earliest period of their history, they have been left with very flawed notions of some of the Divine attributes. This religion has failed to represent the agency of God in the creation and providence, so clearly as to preserve the mass of the nation from grossly erroneous views of the Divine nature and the neglect of prayer.[64]

Edkins connected the Chinese notions of God with morality. While noting the belief in various gods and deities, he attempted to emphasize the importance of God, the foundation of Chinese monotheism. He said that the Chinese belief in one supreme God favored the steady development of moral ideas in people. In regard to the importance of morality and law in modern society, it was his understanding that the connection between moral consciousness and monotheism was clear in Chinese belief and moral consciousness meant the recognition of law, and the law prevailed over humans and influenced their conduct much more powerfully when the thought of the Sovereign Ruler was present. Therefore, the Chinese people have always held the notion of Heaven in their minds so they could differentiate between right and wrong. In this sense, the sanctions of monotheism were much more potent than the sanctions of other (inferior) gods in China. He concluded, "The old religion of China being monotheistic, the moral distinctions are found to be laid down. When the personality of God is obscured, and heaven is thought of as an impersonal power, the moral sense is not destroyed." And "The effect of monotheistic faith on public morality is seen in the ethical purity of Chinese literature."[65]

Edkins also explained the reasons why the Chinese did not accept Christianity. First, Christianity prohibited ancestor worship, which went against the core values of Chinese society and tradition.[66] Second, Christianity, being monotheistic, was exclusive in terms of the acceptance of all other religions and practices.

---

[64] Edkins, *Religion in China*, 94–95. Edkins noted that Buddhism professed atheism, and it denied that there was an eternal God, the creator of the world. He did not distinguish between early Buddhism and Mahayana Buddhism. Mahayana Buddhism developed the theory of the Three Bodies of the Buddhahood so the Buddha (s) could respond to the requests of sentient beings. The same was true of the bodhisattvas.

[65] J. Edkins, "Preface," *The Early Spread of Religious Ideas especially in the Far East* (London: The Religious Tract Society, 1893), 109–110.

[66] W. A. P. Martin expressed the similar idea during the general conference of the Protestant missionaries in Shanghai in 1890. See his "The Worship of Ancestors – A Plea for Toleration," in the Editorial Committee ed., *Records of the General Conference of the Protestant Missionaries in China, Held at Shanghai, May 7–20, 1890* (Shanghai: American Presbyterian Mission Press, 1890), 631.

Third, Christianity was the religion of the foreigners. And fourth, Christianity imitated many Buddhist concepts and rituals.

While most missionary scholars focused on the religions in China, the emergence of comparative religious studies offered new horizons for some missionaries to look into China's religious traditions and other traditions in Asia from a broader perspective.[67] In his textbook for the Unitarian Sunday School Society, *Comparative Studies in Religion*, the minister Henry T. Secrist attempted to discuss religions in China from a broader context of beliefs under the new approach of comparative religious studies. He seemed interested in introducing new concepts for categorizing some of the religious traditions in China, so he made distinctions between the ancient form of religion of the Chinese and Confucianism as a state religion. He claimed that Christianity was the most significant religion in the world and the best because it was the religion of the most progressive peoples and best suited to the needs of modern life.

In contrast, many other religions were not "world" religions. They were "ethnic" religions belonging to one race or nation.[68] In dealing with China, Secrist recognized that "a religion in China" was called "the religion of the Chinese." For him, "An ancient form of religion is shown in the sacred books of the Chinese, a religion without any specific name, but existing before Confucianism, which is now the main religion of the Chinese." Surprisingly, as he was not a well-trained scholar of religions, the sacred books that he was referring to were the Five Books in classical Confucianism: the *Book of Changes* (Yijing), the *Book of History* (Shangshu), the *Book of Odes* (Shijing), the *Book of Ceremonies* (Liji), and the *Spring and Autumn Annals* (Chunqiu). Then he declared, "In the ancient times there seems to have been mainly a belief in one God, *Shangdi*, who was the ruler of earth and heaven, of nations, and persons. But the idea is not distinct."[69] Thus, he attempted to identify *Shangdi* as the One God in China's ancient form of religion by looking for this God in the writings of classical Confucianism. In other words, he believed that these classical Confucian texts preserved the monotheistic belief of ancient religion in China. He noted that this ancient religion was not Confucianism itself because Confucianism was the state religion of the Chinese and was derived from the teachings of Confucius – a scholar, statesman, philosopher, and a sage, who taught

---

[67] For the early studies of comparative religions, especially on Asian religions, see S. H. Kellogg, *The Light of Asia and the Light of the World* (London: Macmillan, 1885); S. H. Kellogg, *A Handbook of Comparative Religion* (Philadelphia: The Westminster Press, 1899).

[68] He was aware that it was sometimes said that there were no deities in Buddhism, but he responded, "But Buddha became himself a deity to his followers, and was worshiped. There are many images of him as a god" (9).

[69] H. T. Secrist, *Comparative Studies in Religion* (Boston: Unitarian Sunday-School Society, 1909), 1–14, especially 13–14.

the rules and regulations for handling affairs of the state and personal and family life relations, as well as the virtues of benevolence, loyalty, truthfulness, justice, and filial piety. When researching the East Asian religions, Secrist could see some commonality among the various traditions. He pointed out that Confucianism, Shintoism, and all forms of the religions of the Chinese shared the worship of ancestors. In short, a monotheistic tradition had developed in the old records of the ancient religion in China and it was preserved in the classical Chinese Confucian texts, but Confucianism itself was a state religion and was different from this old form of ancient religion.

By the early twentieth century, the missionary Sinologists were receiving more intellectual nourishment from various sources. Their understanding of the religions in China and their tireless efforts at seeking monotheism in China became more intense and theoretical. While giving a series of lectures at Queen's College of Oxford University in 1912, Soothill listed four theories regarding the origin of the idea of God in China: the ancestral, the dream or ghost, the animistic, and the innate monotheistic. His classes primarily focused on the Three Teachings in China and especially on the men believed to have founded them: Confucius, Laozi, and the Buddha.[70] He considered Confucianism the state religion and noted that the Imperial state recognized all three religions. Besides these three religions, Soothill addressed some crucial issues on the idea of God in China (particularly in Lecture V), the cosmological arguments, the soul and sin, and ancestor worship. He distinguished between public religion (the official cult) and personal religion.

Soothill divided the four theories on the origin of God in China into two groups: the older one and the modern one. The older one was from Rev. Ross, who asserted that the original religion of the Chinese was monotheism because "we find in the oldest records a belief in a Supreme Ruler, [and] this belief must have been innate in, or co-exited with the Chinese race."[71] Jan J. de Groot represented the modern group and he believed that the primeval form of the religion of the Chinese was animistic.[72] Soothill refuted this:

> the national religion recognizes a Supreme Being, personally denoted by Tian, or Heaven; personally denoted by Shangdi, or the Ruler above, the Over Ruler, or in other words, the Supreme Sovereign. In the invisible world, He is

---

[70] W. E. Soothill, *The Three Religions of China: Lectures Delivered at Oxford* (London and New York: Holder and Stoughton, 1913).

[71] Ross, using the language of Legge, declares in his book that the original religion of the Chinese was monotheistic, though not henotheistic. They "believed in and worshipped a plurality of inferior deities of various grades subordinate to the Supreme God." See W. E. Soothill, *The Three Religions of China*, 125–126.

[72] J. J. M. de Groot, *The Religious System of China* (Leiden: Brill, 1892–1901).

aided by a multitude of spirits or divine beings; in the visible world by sages and rulers, or whom the chief is the Emperor of China, who, as pontifex maximus and vicar of God, has sole right to sacrifice to Him as Shangdi. However, as impersonal Heaven, and even as Shangdi, all men may approach Him.[73]

However, Soothill claimed that these concepts were beyond our knowledge to assert.

As a scholar, Soothill devoted himself to reading the ancient Chinese documents, the standard Confucian classics in his era, including the Five Books and the Four Books.[74] He noted that the oldest book was the *Book of Documents* (Shangshu), or the *Book of History*, and in this book, the first term for God was "*Shangdi*," which referred to the Supreme Being and the Ruler above. In ancient China, around 2300–2200 BCE, the nation's rulers worshipped this Supreme Being and offered the regulation sacrifices to this Supreme Being. Thus, Soothill believed that at the very beginning of recorded history, the leader of the Chinese empire supported a kind of monotheism in the worship of a Supreme Being, the animistic worship of hills and rivers, and the polytheistic worship of a host of spirits.

It was unusual for Soothill to have even learned that the famed explorer Aurel Stein had exhumed numerous materials from a garrison buried in the sand on the northwest frontier of the Chinese empire. He realized that the tablets of wood Stein had brought back to Britain were inscribed with ancient characters, and he claimed that these documents were probably written in the second millennium before Christ. He quickly connected these discoveries in China to a broader backdrop of Asian history. He raised a concern about where the original home of the Chinese civilization was. He questioned this saying, "If they [the Chinese] are not indigenous, but immigrants, then their early notions must be sought elsewhere."[75] This broke new ground for addressing the religious tradition in China in the context of Asia. In the colonial context, some missionaries turned their eyes to the religious traditions on the ancient routes of the Silk Road.

---

[73] Soothill, *The Three Religions of China*, 130.

[74] The most famous translations of the Confucian Four Books often refer to J. Legge's translations in the *Sacred Books of the East*. These four books were translated in the early nineteenth century; see D. Collie, *The Chinese Classical Work Commonly Called the Four Books* (Malacca: Printed at the Mission Press, 1828); other missionaries also translated them and studied them see E. Faber, *A Systematical Digest of the Doctrines of Confucius*, translated from the German by P. G. von Möllendorff (Hong Kong: Printed at the "China Mail" Office, 1875); E. Fabor, *The Mind of Mencius* (Tokyo: Nippon Seikokwai Shuppan Kwaisha, Yokohama, Shanghai, Hong Kong, Singapore: Kelley and Walsh Limited, 1897).

[75] Soothill, *The Three Religions of China*, 131.

4 Chinese Monotheism along the Silk Road and Indo-European Civilizations

4.1 Introduction

As early as the early 1880s, the notable Chinese Buddhist pilgrim Xuanzang's travelogue, *The Records on the Western Regions in the Great Tang* (Da Tang xiyou ji), was translated by Samuel Beal into English, inspiring many Western scholars to conduct archaeological excavations and field investigations in the ancient ruins along the Silk Road.[76] Subsequently, with the expansion of European colonialism in the nineteenth century, numerous Western explorers rushed to the Asian continent in search of antiquities. They uncovered various manuscripts and found amazing artifacts. These newly discovered items were sent to many institutions throughout Europe. They inspired many generations of scholars to decipher the dead languages, read the manuscripts, and study the lost civilizations of Asia. In particular, since the nineteenth century, Western explorers have found the ruins of many ancient cities buried under the sands of Central Asia, and along the old routes of the Silk Road. Countless manuscripts and monuments written in numerous dead languages, especially in Indic and Iranian languages, revealed that there were robust cultural, religious, and material exchanges linking different parts of Asia, from the eastern coast of the Mediterranean to the western coast of the Pacific Ocean.

Although the modern study of Asian religions, such as Zoroastrianism, Buddhism, Manichaeism, Nestorianism, and the East Asian religions, began with the European scholars' intellectual interest in the origin of European civilization, it also aimed to find internal connections among the various Asian religions. In particular, the religious manuscripts and monuments uncovered in China inspired researchers to determine how to evaluate the spread of Indo-Iranian religions to China. Although Buddhism originated in South Asia, many notable first generation Buddhist monks who arrived in China in the first two or three centuries were Indo-European or Indo-Iranian language speakers. They often had Tocharian, Persian, and Sogdian language backgrounds.[77] For example, An Shigao, the first eminent monk whose name appears in the Chinese collection

---

[76] S. Beal, *Si-yu-ki: Buddhist Record of the Western World*, 2 vols. (London: Trübner, 1884). Two years later, J. Legge translated Faxian's travelogue; see *A Record of the Buddhist Kingdoms* (Oxford: Clarendon Press, 1886).

[77] E. Zürcher, *The Buddhist Conquest of China* (Leiden: Brill, 1972); J. McRae and J. Nattier, eds., *Buddhism across Boundaries: Chinese Buddhism and the Western Regions* (Sanchung, Taipei: Fo Guang Shan Foundation, 1999); M. N. Walter, "Tokharian Buddhism in Kucha: Buddhism of Indo-European Centum Speakers in Chinese Turkestan before the 10th Century C.E.," *Sino-Platonic Papers*, 85, 1998; M. N. Walter, "Sogdians and Buddhism," *Sino-Platonic Papers*, 174, November, 2006; F. Grenet, "Religious Diversity among Sogdian Merchants in Sixth-Century China: Zoroastrianism, Buddhism, Manichaeism, and Hinduism," *Comparative Studies of South*

of the *Biographies of Eminent Monks*, was a hostage from Persia.[78] The roles of the Iranian language speakers in the spread of the Central Asian religions to China pushed scholars to think about the inter-Asian cultural links in ancient times. Zoroastrianism, Manicheism, and Nestorianism also travelled along the Silk Road and finally arrived in China. Numerous manuscripts, wall paintings, textiles, and artifacts from these religious traditions have been found in many ancient cities along the Silk Road since the late nineteenth century. In examining these archaeological materials, it is evident that the missionaries or refugees of these three religions who arrived in China mostly came from a Persian or Sogdian background.[79]

4.2 Seeking the Historical Roots of Chinese Monotheism in West Asia

It should be noted that some missionaries have proposed that monotheism in China might have its historical roots in West Asia where the cradle of human civilization developed much earlier. British missionary Sinologist Joseph Edkins developed one of the most exciting hypotheses, tracing the early religious system in China back to the Persian culture. His theory benefited greatly from European philology and archaeological discoveries in Asia. Newly emerging research fields such as Asian historical philology and comparative religions played a significant role in Edkins's journey of seeking the historical development of monotheism from China to Persia across the vast Asian continent.

In 1893, Edkins published a small pamphlet titled *The Early Spread of Religious Ideas, Especially in the Far East*. This is one of the most exciting books on monotheism in China because it compares it with that in Persia. This comparison

---

Asia, Africa and the Middle East, 27: 2 (2007), 463–478; D. N. MacKenzie, *The "Sūtra of the Causes and Effects of Actions" in Sogdian* (London: School of Oriental and African Studies, University of London, 1970); D. N. Mackenzie, *The Buddhist Sogdian Texts of the British Library*, Acta Iranica 10 (Téhéran: Bibliothèque Pahlavi; Leiden: Diffusion, Brill, 1976).

[78] A. Forte, *The Hostage an Shigao and His Offspring: An Iranian Family in China* (Kyoto: Italian School of East Asian Studies, 1995).

[79] R. C. Foltz, *Religions of the Silk Road: Premodern Patterns of Globalization* (New York: Palgrave Macmillan US, 2010); M. Boyce and F. Grenet, *A History of Zoroastrianism*, vol. 3 (Leiden: Brill, 1991); M. Boyce and A. de Jong, *A History or Zoroastrianism*, vol. 4 (Leiden: Brill, 2010); F . Grenet, "L'art zoroastrien en Sogdiane: études d'iconographie funéraire," *Mesopotamia*, 21 (1986), 97–131; F. Grenet and G. Zhang, "The Last Refuge of the Sogdian Religion: Dunhuang in the Ninth and Tenth Centuries," *Bulletin of the Asia Institute*, 10, Studies in Honor of Vladimir Livshits (1998), 175–186; P. Riboud, "La diffusion des religions du monde iranien en Chine entre le VIe et le Xe siècle de notre ère," *Etudes Chinoises*, 24 (2006), 269–284; S. N. C. Lieu, *Manichaeism in the Later Roman Empire and Medieval China: A Historical Survey* (Manchester: Manchester University Press, 1985); S. N. C. Lieu, *Manichaeism in Central Asia and China* (Leiden: Brill, 1998).

is made within the framework of modern European philology in the nineteenth century. This book is a collection of a series of lectures Edkins gave at the Indian Institute, Oxford; at New College, Hampstead; at Cheshunt College; and in the Memorial Hall, Farringdon Street, at a meeting of the London Congregation Union. Under the influence of the growing discipline of European philology, Edkins began to seek the primeval religious history of the human race within the rich collection of Asiatic literature because he believed that "from the first, God communicated His will to His creature man in the form of revelation," and claimed, "In China, India, Tartary, Tibet, and Japan, the early inhabitants when they arrived would retain features of the first revelations imparted to humankind before the days of Noah and Abraham. This we see in the wide range of monotheism in China, Persia, Arabia, and Palestine." Then, Edkins looked for the early history of the idea of God in ancient Oriental languages and literature and tried to demonstrate that the history of languages showed that "mankind began their life on the earth with a common speech, worship, and religion."[80] He also asserted that "the first revelations were made to men who preceded on the chart of time both the Chinese in China and the Akkadians in Babylonia. The Akkadians inherited the tradition of those revelations in Babylonia and the Chinese in China." It was his belief that "The monotheism of China and Persia is a survival of the revelation made to Enoch, Noah, and other primaeval patriarchs."[81]

Following the lead of many European scholars in his era, Edkins always attempted to understand religions by studying languages. He started his argument by tracing the early history of human languages.[82] He first accepted the European scholarship on the Indo-European religious texts. He suggested that writing was first invented in Babylonia about 4000 BCE, and the Egyptians and Chinese followed the Babylonians in developing their writing systems. He also claimed that the Vedas in India were preserved much earlier than the cuneiform writing revelations and sacred history conveyed by oral tradition and that the origins of Hebrew literature seemed to be transcribed and translated from cuneiform documents. As the chief founder, Moses belonged to the early spread of Phoenician writing. Edkins claimed, "If God spoke to man by Adam, Enos, Enoch, and Noah, as Christians believe He did, the truths and duties He taught must exist in some form in the literature of their descendants, among whom are the nations which possess these sacred books (the *Zend-Avesta*, the Vedas, the

---

[80] Edkins, *The Early Spread of Religious Ideas*, 10.
[81] Edkins, *The Early Spread of Religious Ideas*, 10–11.
[82] J. Edkins, "The Evolution of the Chinese Language as Exemplifying the Origin and Growth of Human Speech," *Journal of Peking Oriental Society*, 2: 1 (1887), 1–91; he also had concrete field experience with various religious practices in China that can be found in his "Religious Sects in North China," *The Chinese Recorder and Missionary Journal*, 17: 7 (1886), 245–252.

Chinese sacred books, and the Buddhist sutras)." He continued, "We place the languages in their order. The Hebrew is post-diluvian. The Chinese, the Mongol, and the Tibetan are older. We must extend our chronology sufficiently to allow for the growth of the Mongol, Tibetan, Chinese, and other forms of speech in the Far East. They belong to the antediluvian as well as to the postdiluvian ages."[83] By introducing the early history of some of the most significant writing systems in Asia, Edkins planned to lay the chronological philological foundation for his theory because he believed that the words themselves were key to understanding the religious thinking of the peoples of the ancient world.

Edkins moved on from languages to the history of texts. He turned to the six volumes of Chinese texts translated by James Legge in the *Sacred Books of the East* because they were rich sources of ancient history and poetry of the Chinese and their religious philosophy, rituals, and divination. Edkins's theory is based on his understanding of the connection between Christian theology and Jewish faith and his belief that

> Christian theology suffers if we trace the ancient laws and usages of the Jews to a heathen origin. Suppose, on the other hand. We trace heathen beliefs to a divine origin. In that case, we may hope to aid the Christian cause among intelligent heathens, who will accept our religion more readily when we discover something divine in their own.[84]

Focusing on primeval monotheism in China and Persia, Edkins claimed that the Chinese ideas on God are a valuable witness to the fact that in the earliest times, humans were monotheistic. In a discussion of the oldest Chinese books in which God can be found, Edkins cited the *Book of History* (Shangshu), which reported that the emperor Shun (2300 BCE) offered sacrifices to Shangdi, the Supreme Ruler. Shun also offered "spread-out" sacrifices to the six divinities of the second class. Edkins proposed that the "*Shangdi*" in the Chinese sources was identical with Ahura-Mazda, the highest God in the ancient religion of the Persians.[85] Moreover, he thought that these divinities of the second class could be identified with the spirits who presided over the creation of water, wood, fire, metal, earth, and animals in the Persian religion. Although they were unnamed in the Chinese classics, these divinities were associated with the Amesha

---

[83] Edkins, *The Early Spread of Religious Ideas*, 17–19.
[84] Edkins, *The Early Spread of Religious Ideas*, 21.
[85] For a concise introduction to this god, see W. W. Malandra, *An Introduction to Ancient Iranian Religion: Readings from the Avesta and Achaemenid Inscriptions* (Minneapolis: University of Minnesota Press, 1983), 44–55; M. Boyce, *A History of Zoroastrianism: The Early Period* (Leiden: Brill, 1989), 192–204.

Spentas of the *Zend-Avesta*.[86] Edkins also listed the third class of sacrifices for the four quarters of space and the hills and rivers.

He traced the origins of the Chinese worship back to Persia and stated that the Persian religious ideas were introduced to China as early as the third millennium before Christ. Then he listed eight pieces of evidence:

1) The earliest parts of the Chinese *Book of Divinations* contained the theory of Yin and Yang theory, a dualist philosophy of light and darkness.[87] Similarly, the whole Persian system of religion was built on the dual philosophy of light and darkness.
2) Both ancient Persians and ancient Chinese offered sacrifices on high mountains.
3) Both the Persians and the Chinese thought there were four elemental powers in Nature, as presented in the *Zend-Avesta* and in the *Book of History*. These elements were supposed to be powers moving through Nature and controlling over the various substances named in the books. These ideas about the four outstanding elements in nature differed from those of the Indians and Greeks whose theory contained five elements – metal, trees, water, fire and earth.
4) Human sacrifices were offered in the seventh century BCE following Persian rites in Henan, a central province in northern China. Edkins believed that the Chinese princes from the nomadic tribes might have followed the Persian religion.
5) Across the Asian continent, various groups and tribes constantly practiced the worship of Hormosda, or Ahura-Mazda or Ormuzd, a deity that Elkins thought was worshipped along with the worship of fire and of Buddhism in South Asia. He surmised that this religion was still being practiced in Mongolia and Manchuria even in his time.
6) In the Han Dynasty, before the introduction of Buddhism into China, the Chinese developed a creed about the future state. This creed may have been connected with the worship of the gods of high mountains, the same as that in the Persian religion.
7) This sort of future state was also an article of belief in Japan and Mongolia at the same time.
8) The competition of Zoroastrian religion under Shapur II led to its spread to China. It was given the name of the Chinese faith of the god of fire.[88] Elkins

---
[86] Edkins, *The Early Spread of Religious Ideas*, 22–23.
[87] The so-called *Book of Divinations* here must be the *Book of Changes* (Yijing) since Edkins mentioned that it focused on the Yin-Yang theory. This book was used by ancient Chinese diviners as a guide for their practices.
[88] W. Lin, *Bosi baihuojiao yu gudai Zhongguo* [Zoroastrianism and Ancient China] (Taipei: Xinwenfeng chuban gongsi, 1995); X. Zhang, *Zhonggu huahua xianjiao kaoshu* [A Study of Sinicized Zoroastrianism in Medieval China] (Beijing: Wenwu chubanshe, 2010); G. Zhang, "Revisiting the Zoroastrian Painting in the Tang Dynasty: If the Image Depicted in the Dunhuang

also noted that the Chinese sources had recorded the spread of this religion in the Central Asian kingdoms of Bukhara and Samarqand.

Edkins used his knowledge of Indo-European languages and cultures to discuss each of these pieces of evidence. His primary source on Zoroastrianism was James Darmesteter's book *Introduction and Notes to the Zend-Avesta*. Darmesteter had also translated the *Zend Avesta* for the *Sacred Books of the East* series, and Edkins certainly benefited from that series to familiarize himself with Darmesteter and Legge's translations of the Persian and Chinese texts. However, it should be noted that though Edkins was not an expert, he did not merely accept Darmesteter's arguments. He criticized Darmesteter for failing to see that Zoroaster was not a divinity but a sage, and he attempted to build an analogue between the ancient religion of Persia and that of China. Edkins saw a connection between the early history of Persian religions and China. He asserted, "The Persian dualistic philosophy was in China probably B.C. 2800 and the system of sacrifices to the powers of Nature would follow it and was certainly included in the religion of China about B.C. 2200."[89] He believed that ancestor worship was a Chinese creation since other Asiatic countries did not practice it to the same extent, and that it seemed the Chinese had added ancestral worship to the earlier religion. He thought that orthodox worship was probably older than sun-worship and Sabeanism and much older than the worship of such divinities as Bel, Nebo, Osiris, Zeus, and Mars. Moreover, he supposed that the Hindus and Persians had the same religion because of both Vedic and Persian mythology.

Edkins even suggested that in China, Fuxi began to teach the philosophy of dualism about 2800 BCE. Hence, the Persian and Hindu mythology in the Vedas and *Zend-Avesta* likely dated no earlier than the second millennium BCE. For Edkins, "Mythology is a morbid growth from philosophy, and polytheism is a mistaken understanding of natural phenomena. The primaeval monotheism is the source from which polytheism was, on account of the localizing and individualizing habit into which man is prone to fall, gradually excogitated."[90] He thought that the ideas of the Persians had spread through the work of the magi.[91] The traveling magi introduced magical technology in Babylonian science to many new regions in Central and East Asia. Edkins

---

Manuscript P. 4518 (24) Can Be Identified as Zoroastrian Deities Daēna and Daēva?" *Tang Yanjiu* (Journal of Tang Studies), 3 (1997), 1–17; G. Zhang, "Trois exemples d'influences mazdéennes dans la Chine des Tang," *Études Chinoises*, 13: 1–2 (1994), Mélanges de sinologie offerts à Jacques Gernet, 203–219.

[89] Edkins, *The Early Spread of Religious Ideas*, 26.
[90] Edkins, *The Early Spread of Religious Ideas*, 28–29.
[91] For an overview of magi, see J. Rose, *The Image of Zoroaster: The Persian Mage Through European Eyes* (Ann Arbor: University of Michigan Press, 2000).

noted that the Sun god, Mithra, was used in China as a name for Sunday in the almanacs: the single character *mit* represented Sunday during the Tang dynasty around 900 CE when the Persian astronomers were in office at the Chinese court and made what was called in Chinese the Huihuili (Muslim calendar) for Chinese imperial use. However, Edkins's comments on the Persian astronomic culture were not accurate. The Zoroastrian magi arrived in China early, perhaps in the fifth century. Their images appeared on the panels of many sarcophagi discovered in north China.[92] However, the Persian weekly calendar was indeed also found in a manuscript dated 974 from Dunhuang that was used by Kang Zun, a Sogdian immigrant from Samarqand.[93] However, the Middle Persian name for Sunday, "Yakshambe," had already appeared on the monument of the church of the East ("Nestorianism") in Chang'an in 781.[94] In the Tang dynasty, there was no calendar called the Huihuili – the Islamic calendar was not known to the Chinese until the thirteenth century.[95]

4.3 Monotheism and Revelation in Asia

Based on the shared idea of revelation in the Asian classics, Edkins surmised that there was a shared monotheism across the Asian continent from Persia to China because

---

[92] B. I. Marshak, "The Sarcophagus of Sabao Yu Hong: A Head of the Foreign Merchants (592–598)," *Orientations*, 35 (2004), 57–65; B. I. Marshak, "La thématique sogdienne dans l'art de la Chine de la seconde moitié du VIe siécle," *Comptes rendus des séances de l'année 2001*, (Académie des inscriptions et belles-lettres, Paris, 2001), 227–64; J. A. Lerner, "Aspects of Assimilation: The Funerary Practices and Furnishings of Central Asians in China," *Sino-Platonic Papers*, 168 (December, 2005), 1–65; J. A. Lerner, "Zoroastrian Funerary Beliefs and Practices Known from the Sino-Sogdian Tombs in China," *The Silk Road*, 9 (2011), 18–25.

[93] T. Jao, "Lun Qiyao Yu Shiyiyao" (On Seven Stars and Eleven Stars: On Kang Zun's Commentary on Daily Book from 974), *Xuantang jilin* (Taipei: Mingwen shuju, 1984), 771–793; X. Rong, "Yi ge shi Tangchao de Bosi Jingjiao jiazu [A Nestorian Christian Family Who Served in the Tang Government]," in his *Zhonggu Zhongguo yu wailai wenming* [Medieval China and Foreign Civilizations] (Beijing: Sanlian shudian, 2001), 238–257.

[94] E. C. D. Hunter, "The Persian Contribution to Christianity in China: Reflections in the Xian Fu Syriac Inscriptions," in Dietmar W. Winkler and Tang Li eds., *Hidden Treasures and Intercultural Encounters: Studies on East Syriac Christianity in Central Asia and China* (Berlin: Lit; London: Global), 71–86; R. T. Godwin, *Persian Christians at the Chinese Court: The Xi'an Stele and the Early Medieval Church of the East* (London: I. B. Taurus, 2018), 276. In fact, the Greek, Persian, and Chinese calendars were all used in the monument of the Church of the East in Chang'an; see H. Chen, "Shared Issues in a Shared Textual Community: Buddhism, Christianity and Daoism in Medieval China," in S. N. C. Lieu and G. Thompson eds., *The Church of the East in Central Asia and China* (Turnhout: Brepols, 2020), 93–109.

[95] See J. Needham, *Science and Civilization in China*, vol. 3: Mathematics and the Sciences of the Heavens and the Earth (Cambridge: Cambridge University Press, 1959), 372–376; T. T. Allsen, *Culture and Conquest in Mongol Eurasia* (Cambridge: Cambridge University Press, 2004), 172.

> The resemblance between the idea of revelation in the Bible, in the Zend Avesta, and the *Shujing* (*Book of Documents*) of China, is most striking. In all these three books, God speaks in words to the chosen prophet of an empire. There is also no slight resemblance in the laws of fasting and purification. The religious idea is strikingly similar, so far as faith in monotheism and the character of the religious observances are concerned. The precedence of monotheism and the later introduction of ancestral worship seem to be fair deductions from the facts.[96]

In this sense, again, he used the Western concept of revelation to interpret these ancient Asian religions While aligning the Chinese classic the *Book of Documents* or *Book of History* (Shangshu, Shujing) with the Zoroastrian Avesta and the Bible, Edkins seemed to view the *Book of Documents* as a religious text, as Legge had translated it as a sacred book of the East. However, the nature of this text was arguable from the perspective of modern religious studies.

Edkins also connected primitive monotheism in ancient China with revelations from God to humans since Christianity's concept of revelation was so influential. Citing Legge's translation of the *Book of Odes* (Shijing), he claimed that the poems in this collection demonstrated the verbal revelation from God to King Wen of the Zhou Dynasty.[97] One verse said, "Be not like those who reject this and cling to that. Be not like those ruled by their fancies and desires; I notice your intellectual virtue favorably. You act in accord with God's law. Take measures against the land of your enemy, and with your brothers, prepare scaling-ladders to attack the walls of Zong."[98] The ancient texts developed the political and religious rhetoric in which the Mandate of Heaven (or God) granted power and the throne. Edkins argued that primitive monotheism and early revelation appeared among the Semitic and Chinese peoples based on the evidence he found. Before Buddhism as a cult that worshipped images was introduced to China and the polytheistic teaching "polluted" China, there was indeed a sort of faith in one personal God, who revealed Himself to humans in dreams and outside of them.

Furthermore, Edkins proposed that the monotheistic places already had a sense of right and wrong because monotheism recognized intuitional morality. For him, the monotheistic peoples maintained a comparatively high standard of responsibility.[99] Interestingly, he continued to comment

---

[96] Edkins, *The Early Spread of Religious Ideas*, 30.
[97] King Wen of the Zhou Dynasty was regarded as an ancient sage in the Chinese cultural and political tradition.
[98] J. Legge trans., *Chinese Classics*, vol. iv (Oxford: Clarendon Press, 1861), 452, 454. A challenge toward the philological study can be found in E. Faber, *Introduction to the Science of Chinese Religion* (Hong Kong: Lane, Crawford, 1879).
[99] Edkins, *The Early Spread of Religious Ideas*, 32.

on the historical development of revelations by divine beings in China. For example, in fourth-century Daoism, Laozi and some of the other saints had revealed the words of God to humans.[100] Edkins also asserted that the early physical philosophy of the *Book of Changes* was of Persian origin, which was free from polytheism and was similar to the religion of the Aryans who derived purer and more correct ideas from the Babylonian civilization. Therefore, in Edkin's eyes, comparatively pure and elevated thought must have existed among all the more enlightened Aryan nations. Persia, before Zoroaster, had a long history of a monotheistic religion. A budding dualistic philosophy prevailed later, similar to the religious developments in Chinese history. Edkins concluded, "Through the effect of early revelation, the conception of a God is universal among men, except when by vice, isolation, and bad teaching the idea becomes obscured. God being universally known, He can be named differently by this and that race, but He is the same to all men. He is one being."[101] According to his understanding, the Chinese character "*di*" referred to "ruler" and "emperor," as well as God in ancient Chinese history because the Chinese conceived God as a sovereign. The Chinese thus developed solid political ideas of social and moral importance.

Edkins emphasized the universality of the idea of God across all Asia in ancient times. He suggested that in an international etymology, the Aryan, Hebrew, and Chinese languages embraced the ideas of brightness, sovereignty, and power in the early conception of God as Deus, Elohim, and *Di*, respectively). The Aryans, Persians, and Chinese were all originally monotheists, and later they were all in connected by a philosophy of dualism. These shared ideas were earlier than the Hindu philosophy and mythology in Greece and Western Asia. As Edkins stressed, there was no mythology in the Chinese classics of divination and history, only monotheism and a dualist philosophy.

5 From Monotheism to Polytheism in Chinese History

5.1 Introduction

As early as the seventeenth century, based on their experience in China, the first generation of Jesuit missionaries realized that the Chinese worshipped multiple gods and deities rather than just one God. Matteo Ricci said that the

---

[100] For the study of revelations in Daoism, see M. Strickmann, "The Mao Shan Revelations: Taoism and the Aristocracy," *T'oung Pao* 2nd Series, 63: 1 (1977), 1–64; I. Robinet, *Taoist Meditation: The Mao-Shan Tradition of Great Purity*, translated by Julian F. Pas, Norman J. Girardot (Albany: State University of New York Press, 1979); S. R. Bokenkamp, *A Fourth-Century Daoist Family: The Zhen'gao, Or Declarations of the Perfected*, vol. 1 (Berkeley: University of California Press, 2020).

[101] Edkins, *The Early Spread of Religious Ideas*, 36.

religion of ancient China was monotheistic, but later, the worship of multiple gods appeared. The Jesuit belief in the degeneration from monotheism to polytheism in Chinese history was passed on when the Protestant missionaries started their enterprise in China in the nineteenth century. For example, Bishop James W. Bashford stated in his book *China: An Interpretation* that there was monotheism in ancient China, but later polytheism dominated.[102]

The missionaries attempted to identify monotheism in the Chinese religious traditions to convert the Chinese. However, once they found themselves in China, they had to face the challenge that most Chinese worshipped multiple gods and deities. Besides the standardized Buddhist and Daoist gods and deities and the ancestral cults, there was also the worship of animals, rivers, mountains, and other aspects of nature. George Smith was among the first-generation missionaries to enter China after the Opium War. He left a detailed account of the concrete religious practices in South China. He saw numerous Buddhist and Daoist temples in Canton, where the Buddhist temples accounted for the majority, but he also noted that a significant number were dedicated to the temples of the ancestors. Therefore, he called this "universal idolatry."[103] John Henry Gray (1828–1890) also suggested the idea of God in ancient China, but this monotheism was disrupted with the introduction of Buddhism and Daoism and their new gods and deities that competed with monotheism. Many heroes were deified, and the gods of wealth, war, and longevity were created for worship.[104]

5.2 Monotheism's Degeneration into Polytheism across Asia

Joseph Edkins noticed that this degeneration happened in China and India as well as in many empires and kingdoms of the East. For him, the idea of God became trinitarian in China and India. There were three major gods in Buddhism and Daoism that were worshipped by the local people. Later, the religious thought in both India and China became polytheistic and more gods were worshipped. He attributed the degeneration to the spread of mythology, which resulted in idolatry. Therefore, he thought that a process of deterioration had commenced after monotheism had existed, probably for some centuries.[105]

Edkins examined what polytheism meant in Chinese history and traced its origin to foreign sources. He noted that monotheism appeared along with

---

[102] X. Lian, *The Conversion of Missionaries: Liberalism in American Protestant Missions in China, 1907–1932* (University Park, PA: Pennsylvania State University Press, 1997), 179.

[103] G. Smith, *A Narrative of an Exploratory Visit to Each of the Consular Cities of China* (New York: Harper & Brothers, 1847), 31.

[104] J. H. Gray, *China* (London: Macmillan, 1878; Mineola, NY: Dover, 2002, reprinted), 75, 99.

[105] Edkins, *The Early Spread of Religious Ideas*, 59.

ancestor worship, the practice of divination, and the philosophy of dualism. With the growth of the worship of the spirits of nature and ancestral worship, polytheism began to replace monotheism. Just as he saw a shared sense of monotheism in ancient Persia and China, he saw the same degeneration from monotheism to polytheism among the Babylonians and the Chinese due to the growth of mythology. He even suggested that a form of Mesopotamian mythology mixed with Chaldean astrology had entered China sometime in the eighth to tenth centuries BCE. This mythology led the Chinese to begin to naming and worshipping many deities.[106] Edkins traced how divination in ancient China developed because it was a degraded form of the earlier revelations of God. His interpretation was that in the ancient monotheistic age, there were already people who could not understand the revelations of God, so they had to consult religious teachers and they received answers from God through conferring with these diviners – and this was the origin of divination.

Edkins also traced the origins of worshipping animals and stars. He understood that the Chinese practiced the worship of animals even in his era. For example, he found that the worship of the toad, the snake, the weasel, and the fox was widespread in North China because these animals likely caused damage that affected the local economies, especially agriculture and commerce. However, he tried to understand the origin from a broader context. He found a conception of God in both Egyptian zoological mythology and Chinese mythology. But this monotheistic belief seemed to have metamorphosed into animal worship. For instance, in China, the philosopher Zhuangzi mixed philosophy with metempsychosis.[107] Later, some people regarded the fox, the weasel, and many other animals as gods possessing the divine power of transformation. Moreover, star worship was not practiced by the Chinese in Edkin's time, although he thought that the Buddhists were trying to maintain the worship of the goddess of the Seven Stars.

Williams Dean also believed that the forefathers of the Chinese retained some correct ideas of the true God in ancient times, and they were not worshippers of images. Still, the true God was lost amid the polytheism that succeeded monotheism. The Chinese started to worship Heaven and earth as the progenitors of the race and the protectors of humans. Gradually the Chinese worshipped even more images and objects. Their gods not only included Heaven and the earth but also

---

[106] Edkins, *The Early Spread of Religious Ideas*, 61–62.
[107] For an early study of Zhuangzi and his philosophy, see F. H. Balfour, *The Divine Classic of Nanhua* (Shanghai: Kelly and Walsh, 1881).

gods of the sun, moon and stars – gods of the rains, wind and seasons – gods of the rivers and the lakes – gods of the mountains and the meadows – gods of the thunder and the lightning – gods of the fire and the furnace – gods of wealth and war – gods of the city and the country – gods of mechanics and merchandise – gods of agriculture and literature – gods of every profession and each pursuit – the goddess of heaven and the goddess of the seas – the goddess of mercy and the demon of misery.[108]

This was the process of moving from monotheism to polytheism.

William A. P. Martin proposed a theory of "historical development or corruption" of the primitive beliefs of the Chinese and attributed it to the institutionalized religions in China. In April 1869, he published an essay on the three religions of China in the *New Englander*. Martin noted that the Chinese primitive beliefs had contact with other exotic systems, including Buddhism, "Mahometanism" (Islam), and Christianity, so foreign elements affected or modified the indigenous Chinese creeds. In Martin's time, the Chinese were what he termed "polytheistic and idolatrous." They worshipped various gods and deities, such as Guanyin, the city gods, and Confucius. He noted that in ancient China the Chinese had the concept of *Shangdi*, the Supreme Ruler. By examining the images of *Shangdi* in old Chinese classical books, he suggested that ancient Chinese writings never depicted the god in a human form or debased by human passions like the Greek god Zeus. He cited a sentence from the *Book of Odes* that addressed the issue of God having no voice or smell, saying that God was imperceptible to the senses. He concluded that "the early Chinese were by no means destitute of the knowledge of God. They did not, indeed, know him as the Creator, but they recognized him as a supreme in providence and without beginning or end."[109] However, he noted that *Shangdi* was already in the first stage of "decay" in the ancient Chinese classics.

Martin went on to discuss how the three religions of China had replaced the ancient idea of God. He argued that Confucius led his followers to the opposite extreme – skepticism – because he ignored the immortality of the soul and the existence of a personal God. Martin traced how Confucius replaced *Shangdi* with the vague appellation *Tian*, which opened the way for atheism that infected Confucian philosophy. Martin asserted that Confucius often discouraged his pupils from finding the answers about a future state, and the goal of the Confucian system was not the truth but expediency. Martin continued to compare Confucius with Jesus Christ. For him,

---

[108] W. Dean, *The Chinese Mission* (New York: Sheldon, 1859), 51–52.

[109] W. A. P. Martin, *Hanlin Paper or Essays on the Intellectual Life of the Chinese* (London: Trübner and Shanghai: Kelley & Walsh Limited, 1880), 130–31.

Jesus Christ appealed to evidence and challenged inquiry, and this characteristic of our religion has shown itself in the mental development of Christian nations.... Confucius selected disciples who should be the depositories of his teachings; Christ chose apostles who should be witnesses of his actions. Confucius died lamenting that the edifice he had labored so long to erect was crumbling to ruin. Christ's death was the crowning act of his life; and his last words, "It is finished."[110]

For Martin, although Confucianism stood out as the leading religion of the Chinese empire in his (Martin's) time, it had degenerated into a pantheistic medley. It rendered worship to an impersonal *anima mundi* under the ultimate forms of visible nature.

Muirhead also pointed out that the Three Teachings were responsible for the degeneration from monotheism to polytheism in China. He claimed that in the earliest classics, there was "a constant allusion to a Divine Being, bearing the name of Shangdi, or Supreme Ruler. Attributes and perfections are ascribed to Him, which are predicative only of the one living and true God, while there is nothing ever hinted of a kind derogatory to Him in this respect."[111] Therefore he concluded that monotheism was the original creed of the Chinese nation. However, he was also a believer that later there was a process of corruption or perversion of the actual truth because God's peculiar and personal character was gradually lost sight of, and Heaven alone or Heaven and earth together were regarded as the supreme objects of nature and spoken of accordingly. He suggested that Confucius had led the way to the deviations from the truth. Eventually, the idea of the Supreme Ruler or *Shangdi* in the ancient teachings passed from view. Muirhead also argued that Buddhism and Daoism extended their influence and introduced numerous objects of worship. Although he realized that the original Daoism had no idolatry or superstition, it later became notorious for its idolatry. The Supreme Ruler and the spiritual beings eventually became idols and were placed under Laozi in the Daoist Pantheon.[112] Confucianism, Buddhism, and Daoism all replaced the original monotheism with numerous idols.

Muirhead was frustrated that there was no detailed account of the act of creation in the Chinese classics. The terms "God" and "Heaven" were also used interchangeably, so there was confusion among ancient people. He discussed how Confucianism used the word and concept of the Great Extreme (*Taiji*), and Daoism used Pangu to discuss the origin of the myriad things. However, he understood that these discussions in the Chinese classics

---

[110] Martin, *Hanlin Paper or Essays*, 140–141.
[111] W. Muirhead, *China and the Gospel* (London: James Nisbet, 1870), 80.
[112] Muirhead, *China and the Gospel*, 83–84.

were different from the work of creation in Christianity since "there is none as to the ways of Providence."

Soothill also expressed his concerns about the degeneration of Confucianism. While preaching the gospel in Wenzhou, he published a book titled *A Mission in China* in 1907.[113] By his time there were already many available books and other writings on Chinese religions and culture. As he noted in the preface to his book, he had benefited from many notable works on religions of China by his contemporary scholars, such as Williams's the *Middle Kingdom*, Legge's *Religions of China* and *Chinese Classics*, Canon MacClatchie's *Chinese Cosmogony* and *Yih King*, Eitel's *Lectures on Buddhism*, Monier Williams's *Buddhism*, and Balfour's *Chwang-tsz*.

Soothill also blamed Daoism and Buddhism for leading monotheism in ancient China to polytheism because those religions introduced numerous gods and saints. He claimed,

> Neither Taoism nor Buddhism has added anything of value to the ancient Chinese idea of God, but, contrariwise, brought about its degradation. They are mainly responsible for the immense multiplication of "gods" or "saints" whom the people ignorantly worship and who have become a dark cloud obscuring God and hiding Him from their dulled vision. The heterogeneity of polytheism has destroyed a search after the material and spiritual homogeneity or unity of the universe, which both faith and experience reveal to the truly enlightened as expressed in the Godhead.[114]

Interestingly, though he acknowledged Confucianism as the state religion of China, he made a distinction between two kinds of Confucianism: ancient and modern. Modern Confucianism was different from the old form of Confucianism because ancient Confucianism reflected the teachings of the Master, Confucius.[115] For Soothill, ancient Confucianism recognized the existence of a Supreme Being, who was called *Shen* or *Di*, or more often *Shangdi*, the Ruler Above or Over, which was indicted by the impersonal *Tian*, Heaven. It was only the emperor, the Son of Heaven, who could make sacrifices to this *Shangdi* or Heaven and the emperor offered the sacrifices in the Imperial Temple of Heaven. These sacrifices might have included silk, grain, jade, sheep, pigs, and other small animals, as well as a burnt offering of a whole bullock. There was no idol at the sacrifices, only a spirit tablet of *Shangdi* – a strip of wood with the great name inscribed on it. Soothill also

---

[113] W. E. Soothill, *A Mission in China* (Edinburgh and London: Oliphant, Anderson & Ferrier, 1907).

[114] Soothill, *A Mission in China*, 151.

[115] On the evolving understanding of Confucianism among the Jesuit missionaries and the confrontation between China and the West, see L. M. Jensen, *Manufacturing Confucianism: Chinese Traditions and Universal Civilization* (Durham: Duke University Press, 1998).

noted that there was no image of Confucius that was worshipped in ancient times. Therefore, he suggested that idolatry was absent in this ancient form of Confucianism. He attributed the making of idols to the advent of Buddhism. However, he realized that the imperial worship was by no means monotheistic because the emperor also worshipped many other divinities besides Heaven and earth. He offered sacrifices in various temples to the spirits of the hills and rivers, the spirits controlling such elements as rain and snow, fire and thunder, the sun, moon, stars, his ancestors, and folk heroes.[116]

American scholar F. Brinkley further explained China's degeneration from monotheism to polytheism. Following the lead of the acclaimed missionary Sinologist James Legge, he focused on analyzing the ancient Chinese language and writing from a philological perspective. Brinkley maintained that the early religion of China about five thousand years ago was monotheism focused worshipping Heaven, God (*Di*), and the August God (*Huangdi*). According to Brinkley, although these words had different meanings, there was no doubt that "Heaven" in the Chinese mind referred to the incredible power that ruled the universe. Furthermore, he traced the historical development of the Chinese word "emperor," which he saw as the personification of Heaven. He examined the titles of the temple shrines for the deceased emperors in Chinese history and noticed that in about the third century BCE, some of the early rulers also received the posthumous title of "emperor" because of the sacrifices that were offered to their spirit shrines in the imperial family temples. He referred to this process as the secularization of imperial thinking. This, he claimed, became a source of misunderstanding the ancient Chinese religions by theologians because the spirit above was called "God" and the energy on the earth was referred to as "deities."[117] He also looked into the animistic tendencies and superstitious divination that influenced monotheism in ancient China.

5.3 Monotheism and Idolatry in Chinese Religions

Among the many forms of idolatry, ancestor worship and the sacrificial rites for the ancestors troubled the missionaries the most. In addition, the apostles were frustrated with the endless polytheistic beliefs. These gods developed into various cults. The Chinese sacrificed to many different gods and cults in the Confucian, Buddhist, and Daoist traditions. For example, DuBose listed many divinities in Confucianism,[118] such as the God of Wenchang, the Star-Lord, Lord Guan, the

---

[116] Soothill, *A Mission in China*, 238–239.

[117] F. Brinkley, *China: Its History, Arts, and Literature*, vol. 11, (Boston and Tokyo: J. B. Millet Company, 1902), 43–44; chapters 2–4 on Chinese religions; 38–162.

[118] A. H. Smith, *Chinese Characteristics*, 4th ed., revised, with illustrations (New York: Fleming H. Revell Company, 1894), chapter 26 discusses polytheism, pantheism, and atheism. See also

gods of the five planets, the five sovereignties, the god of the door, the god of the window, and the gods of agriculture, the god of tides, the god of the Classics, the god of writing, the earth god, and the city god. Many of these gods were studied in detail by later generations of China scholars. Some of these gods are no longer regarded as Confucian gods and deities; they are categorized either as gods of popular religion or Daoist deities. In contemporary scholarship on Chinese religions, one of the most popular theories for interpreting the Chinese pantheon is the bureaucratic model, viewing the gods and deities as mirroring the hierarchical bureaucrats of the Chinese empire, as some anthropologists have suggested.[119]

DuBose also listed many Buddhist gods and deities, such as Dipamkara Buddha, the Naga Kings of the Four Seas, Celestial King Li Holding a Tower, Nezha, and the bodhisattvas.[120] DuBose also listed many gods of the masses.[121] S. H. Chester argued that ancestor worship was part of all the Three Teachings.[122] Jas Johnston noted that, in general, Chinese people had very little knowledge of Confucianism as a religion, and most of them simply regarded it as ancestor worship. The average Chinese person may not have known that the emperor of China made sacrifices to Heaven twice a year in the name of offering sacrifices to God. For ordinary people, ancestor worship may have been a true religion, while the gods were beings that the people both respected and feared. In people's eyes,

---

H. C. DuBose, *Religions of Mission Fields as Viewed by Protestant Missionaries* (New York: Student Volunteer Movement for Foreign Missions, 1905).

[119] This theory was laid the foundation by A. P. Wolf in his "Gods, Ghosts, and Ancestors," in A. P. Wolf ed., *Religion and Ritual in Chinese Society* (Stanford: Stanford University Press, 1978), 131–182.

[120] Many of these gods have been studied by Chün-fang Yü, Meir Shahar and other scholars, such as Guanyin and Nezha; see Chün-fang Yü, *Kuan-yin: The Chinese Transformation of Avalokiteśvara* (New York: Columbia University Press, 2001); Meir Shahar, *Oedipal God: The Chinese Nezha and His Indian Origins* (Honolulu: University of Hawai'i Press, 2008).

[121] J. J. M. de Groot (1854–1921), *The Religious System of China*, 6 volumes (Leiden: E. J. Brill, 1892–1910); J. Watson, "Standardizing the Gods: The Promotion of T'ien Hou Along the South China Coast, 960–1960," in D. Johnson et al., *Popular Culture in Late Imperial China* (Berkeley: University of California Press, 1985), 292–324; M. Strickmann, *Chinese Magical Medicine* (Stanford: Stanford University Press, 2002); R. von Glahn, *The Sinister Way: The Divine and the Demonic in Chinese Religious Culture* (Berkeley: University of California Press, 2004); P. Katz, *Images of the Immortal: The Cult of Lu Dongbin at the Palace of Eternal Joy* (Honolulu: University of Hawaii Press, 2000); R. Hymes, *Way and Byway: Taoism, Local Religion, and Models of Divinity in Sung and Modern China* (Berkeley: University of California Press, 2002); E. L. Davis, *Society and the Supernatural in Song China* (Honolulu: University of Hawai'i Press, 2001); J. Lagerway, *Taoist Ritual in Chinese Society and History* (New York: Macmillan, 1987); K. Dean, *Taoist Ritual and Popular Cults of Southeast China* (Princeton: Princeton University Press, 1993); D. Gardner, "Ghosts and Spirits in the Sung Neo-Confucian World: Chu Hsi on kuei-shen," *Journal of the American Oriental Society*, 115: 4 (1995), 598–611.

[122] S. H. Chester, *Lights and Shadows of Mission Work in the Far East: Being the Record of Observation Made during a Visit to the Southern Presbyterian Missions in Japan, China, and Korea in the Year of 1897* (Richmond, VA: The Presbyterian Committee of Publication, 1899).

these gods gave punished people more heavily when they committed bad deeds than they rewarded them for good deeds.[123] Johnston believed that offering sacrifices to the ancestors was indeed a kind of idolatry. He thought that enlightened Chinese might distinguish between offering sacrifices to ancestors and God. He also pointed out that ancestor worship harmed women because the primary responsibility for ancestor worship lay with the son, which meant that having a son was extremely important and when a wife failed to bear a son, it often led to divorce or the husband taking a second wife or concubine. Under Confucianism, some fathers only valued their sons, and many abandoned their daughters. The missionaries realized that their duty was to help save these abandoned children.[124] Ernst Faber also noted that ancestor worship led every Chinese family to raise sons, and men even married concubines to bear sons.[125] Christian missionaries generally believed that Confucianism lacked the universal love of Christianity, and Mozi's theory of universal love only made a minor contribution.[126] Therefore, the missionaries attributed the monotheism's degeneration to polytheism to the decline of Confucian morality.

Although the missionaries blamed the Three Teachings for corrupting monotheism, they were also surprised that all three could coexist.[127] As H. C. DuBose observed, the Confucianists were the literati class, and yet they also worshipped in Buddhist temples and performed Daoist rituals. He was stunned to find that "China is the only country in the world where three systems could stand side-by-side without one expelling or superseding the other."[128] It was difficult for a European missionary to understand how a Chinese person could belong to three religions

---

[123] J. Johnston, *China and Formosa: The Story of the Mission of the Presbyterian Church of England* (London: Harzell, Watson, & Viney, Ld., 1897), 48–67.

[124] Johnston, *China and Formosa*, 50–53.

[125] E. Faber, *Chronological Handbook of the History of China*. A Manuscript left by the late Rev. Ernst Faber. Edited by Pastor Paul Kranz (Shanghai: Published by the General Evangelical Protestant Missionary Society of Germany, printed at the American Presbyterian Mission Press, 1902), ii.

[126] D. Z. Sheffield, "The Ethics of Christianity and of Confucianism Compared," *The Chinese Recorder and Missionary Journal*. Vol. 18 (Shanghai: American Presbyterian Mission Press, 1886), 365–379.

[127] For a contemporary discussion on the co-existence of three teachings in China, see S. F. Teiser, "Introduction: The Spirits of Chinese Religion," in D. S. Lopez ed., *Religions of Asia in Practice: An Anthology* (Princeton: Princeton University Press, 2018), 295–329.

[128] H. C. DuBose, *Dragon, Image, and the Demon: Or the Three Religions of China, Confucianism, Buddhism, and Taoism, giving an Account of the Mythology, Idolatry, and Demonolatry of the Chinese* (London: S. W. Partridge, 1886; New York: A. C. Armstrong), 28–29. P. Zagorin argues that the ideas and practice of the religious tolerance in the West was the heritage of some marginal Protestant Christians. Due to their non-mainstream status in the Western society, they faced the challenges brought up by the dominant Catholic church and the mainstream Protestant church, so they developed the idea of the religious freedom of conscience and tolerance for their survival. See P. Zagorin, *How the Idea of Religious Tolerance Came to the West* (Princeton: Princeton University Press, 2003), 289–311.

simultaneously, yet this was the case with the Chinese. According to DuBose's understanding, Confucianism mainly was based on morality, Buddhism on idolatry, and Daoism on superstition.[129] So Confucianism dealt more with the dead past, Buddhism with the changing future, while Taoism was occupied with the evils of the present. In their relations to philosophy, these three systems focused on ethical, physical, and metaphysical issues, respectively. DuBose noted that these three religions were all supported by the state authority.[130] The problems DuBose had with the three were mainly due to his understanding of modern religion from a Christian perspective. For example, he insisted that Confucianism was not strictly a religion simply because it had no Creator. He had a total lack of desire to come to a real understanding of these three teachings, as none of these three teachings produced a healthy state of religious sentiment.[131] So he concluded that the peaceful coexistence established between the Three Teachings was only possible because they were not true religions.

6 Chinese Religions: The Protestant Heritage in the Twentieth and Twenty-First Centuries

It is clear that the Western missionaries in the nineteenth century carried on some of the legacies of the Jesuit missionaries. They were inclined to identify monotheism in the ancient form of the Chinese religion by referring to the meaning and implication of several key terms in the Chinese classical texts, such as "*di*" (Thearch), "*Shangdi*" (Sovereign on High), and "*Tian*" (Heaven)." They suggested that these terms could be identical to "God" in the Christian

---

[129] DuBose, "Taoism," in *Religions of Mission Fields as Viewed by Protestant Missionaries* (Student Volunteer Movement for Foreign Missions, 1905), 161–181; for a Catholic comprehensive account of so-called superstitions in China, see H. Doré, *Recherches sur les Superstitions en Chine*. 18 vols. translated by D. J. Finn; v. 13 translated by L. F. McGreal (Shanghai, 1911–1938, reprinted in 1966, Ch'eng-wen Publishing Company, Taipei).

[130] In premodern China, while dealing with the religious affairs, the secular court often granted honorific titles to the deceased ministers and generals and approved their offices in the heavenly court. C. K. Yang addresses this issue from the sociological perspective and regards this mode as the state control of religion; see his *Religion in Chinese Society: A Study of Contemporary Social Functions of Religion and Some of their Historical Factors* (Prospect Heghts, IL: Waveland Press, 1991), 180–217. And for the more recent scholarship on the state-religion relationship, see Y. Ashiwa and D. L. Wank eds., *Making Religion, Making the State: The Politics of Religion in Modern China* (Stanford: Stanford University Press, 2009).

[131] American Presbyterian missionary J. L. Nevius (1829–1893), who was familiar with Legge's translations of Chinese Classics and had also learned about Edkins's works, however, found that although Confucianism gave to the Chinese no religion and Chinese literati were usually atheists or pantheists, there was "evidence in the very earliest period of Chinese history a desire to search out the principles of absolute and eternal truth, and an ability to a certain extent to do so." See his book *China and the Chinese* (New York: Harper & Brothers, 1869), 148. Nevius also stated that there was no word for one supreme overruling deity in either Chinese language or literature, though the meaning of "*Tian*" (Heaven) was nearly akin to that of God (*China and the Chinese*, 158).

sense, which laid the spiritual foundation for converting the Chinese to Christianity.[132] Furthermore, combining textual evidence and field experience, these missionaries realized that the Chinese worshipped numerous gods and offered sacrifices to various cults besides God.[133] Therefore, they saw monotheism as clouded by these idolatries and superstitions, making conversion of the Chinese a challenging task for the missionaries.

Moreover, through Indo-European philology and comparative religious studies, some missionaries examined the cultural and spiritual connections and similarities between the Chinese and Persian religions and argued that the Chinese and the Persians shared some religious views. The missionaries thought that they had all believed in monotheism in the earliest times, but that it was lost over the ages. Many missionaries also explained how the Chinese religions had "degenerated" from monotheism to polytheism. They indicated that Confucianism, as a state religion, along with Buddhism and Daoism, had introduced various cults to the original form of monotheism, eventually corrupting it. It should be noted that most of these discussions of monotheism took place in the nineteenth century. In contrast, the missionaries faced different challenges in China in the early twentieth century, so they gradually shifted their focus to other issues. Nevertheless, these debates and discussions on monotheism in Chinese religions laid the foundation in the Western humanities for studying Chinese religions.

In the late nineteenth and early twentieth centuries, the political, religious, and cultural order of the Chinese empire was challenged by many modern ideologies, such as imperialism, colonialism, and nationalism. Both Catholicism and Protestant Christianity were firmly established in many parts of China. Missionaries across the empire operated numerous schools and modern forms of higher education for training civil servants, and professional labor force gradually replaced the old educational system based on the core values of Confucianism. A process of secularization began with the decline of Confucianism as the state ideology and moral foundation of the old empire of China. Many Confucian, Buddhist, and Daoist temples were converted to schools for modern education in the first two decades of the twentieth century. Christianity was also involved in intellectual and cultural conflicts. In the 1920s, some Chinese literati also launched a political and cultural campaign against Christianity that was

---

[132] S. Liu suggests that the only ancient Chinese philosophical school that took seriously the idea of a supreme personal God was the Mohist school ("Theism from a Chinese Perspective," *Philosophy East and West*, 28: 4 (1978), 413–414).

[133] Edkins's wife Jane observed many rituals across China, such as praying for rain; see J. R. Edkins, *Chinese Scenes and People* (London: James Nisbet, 1863).

part of what we would now call a "decolonization" movement.[134] In this context, the debate on monotheism was not much of a concern for the missionaries. Instead, many of them were devoted to the broader study of Chinese society, as was manifested by the activities of YMCA activists in Beijing and elsewhere, who were under the influence of the social gospel movement back in the United States.[135] I would argue that this demonstrated a shift from seeking the theological truth to sociological truth in China.

With the decline of Confucianism as the state religion, the Protestant missionaries also lost their counterpart for discussing on their monotheistic advocation. As many missionaries observed in the nineteenth century, Confucianism certainly played a central role in the official political ideology of the court for much of China's history. Many Confucian values were widely accepted by the literati, officials, and the masses. In 1905, the Qing empire abandoned the civil examination system, and Confucianism was no longer the basis for educating Chinese students and preparing them to serve in the government. But the idea of Confucianism as the state religion still impacted the Chinese intellectuals after the Qing empire collapsed and China moved into the Republican era. In 1915, when the warlord Yuan Shikai proclaimed himself emperor of China, he officially reinstituted Confucianism as the state religion to serve his newly founded Chinese empire. However his kingdom and the reinstatement of Confucianism as the state religion only survived for several months.

Modern nationalism earned some credibility among the Chinese intellectual and political activists in the early twentieth century due to the turbulent political situation in the Qing empire. Western missionaries distinguished between "world religions" and "national religions," which became an issue for some thinkers and activists in Asia who were concerned about national identity. Buddhism was the first non-Abrahamic religion and the first non-monotheistic religion to be recognized as a world religion by the Western missionaries in the late nineteenth century.[136] As Philip C. Almond noted, British scholars attempted to discover

---

[134] T. Yamamoto and S. Yamamoto, "The Anti-Christian Movement in China, 1922–1927," *The Far Eastern Quarterly*, 12:2 (1953), 133–147; P. A. Cohen, "The Anti-Christian Tradition in China," *Journal of Asian Studies*, 20: 2 (February 1961), 169–180; J. G. Lutz, "Chinese Nationalism and the Anti-Christian Campaigns of the 1920s," *Modern Asian Studies*, 10: 3 (1976), 395–416.

[135] For example, some American college students based at Yenching University started carrying out sociological surveys in Beijing; see Y. Chiang, *Social Engineering and the Social Sciences in China, 1919–1949* (New York: Cambridge University Press, 2001).

[136] T. Masuzawa, *The Invention of World Religions: Or, How European Universalism Was Preserved in the Language of Pluralism* (Chicago: University of Chicago Press, 2005), 24; R. King, *Orientalism and Religion: Post-Colonial Theory, India and "The Mystic East"* (London: Routledge, 1999), 64–72. On the discussion on Confucianism as a World religion,

Buddhist tradition by reading and analyzing the ancient texts, which led to a reconstruction of textual Buddhism. However, this textual Buddhism was different from the Buddhist doctrines and practices that the British colonists and missionaries had witnessed in South Asia. From their observations, these colonists and missionaries believed that Buddhism was a declining religion, and this became the ideological foundation for spreading Protestant Christianity in South Asia.[137] Yet in the later part of the nineteenth century, British scholars and writers began to debate whether Buddhism was a religion or a philosophical tradition. Some believed that Buddhism was a form of atheism and a rational teaching, compared with Protestant Christianity.[138] The concept of world religion was connected with the Western idea of universalism that supported Christianity as a universal value system for all nations. With the political decline of the Qing empire and the expansion of Western colonialism, China faced the challenge of building a modern nation-state, at least in the minds of some Chinese thinkers and politicians such as Sun Yat-sen. China did have a brief history of developing a nation-state in the 1910s and 1920s after the collapse of the Chinese empire. Sun and other Chinese leaders tried to establish a new republic that would bring the five major nationalities together and lead to China being recognized as a modern nation.

Beginning with the New Cultural Movement in 1917, some leading Chinese intellectuals under the influence of modern cultural nationalism tried to develop a national (vernacular) Han language and literature and they even to tried to establish Confucianism as the national religion. The Chinese nation-state began to implement the vernacular Han language as a common language for all citizens of the newly founded republic. This language, Mandarin, developed by the intellectuals and instituted by the state government, has been gradually accepted as the national language and used to replace the many local dialects across China. It has been used mainly by Han nationality, the majority nationality in China. The replacement process of this language is similar to that of the sacrificial rites and ceremonies in the imperial era when the court instituted some Confucian sacrificial rites and traditions organized by experts on the Confucian rites based on the Confucian classics, and they implemented them in local areas to replace unauthorized local cultic practices. Some Christian missionaries regarded these centralized and authorized rites and ceremonies as the "Chinese religion."

See A. Sun, *Confucianism as a World Religion: Contested Histories and Contemporary Realities* (Princeton University Press, 2013).

[137] P. C. Almond, *The British Discovery of Buddhism* (Cambridge: Cambridge University Press, 1988), 40.

[138] King, *Orientalism and Religion*, 35–61.

The newly reformed Nationalist Party and the developing Communist Party both claimed to launch a national revolution against feudalism, imperialism, and colonialism. This ideology carried China through the Anti-Japanese War (the post-1941 Pacific War) and the civil war (1945–1949). With the founding of the People's Republic of China in 1949, the Chinese state again went back to the era of empire in the sense that communism was not a national but an international ideology. However, the national independence discourse was still part of the official ideology.

Like Buddhism, Confucianism was a non-monotheistic ideology, and its influence was not limited to one nation. Whether it could be a world religion or a national religion remained a question. In traditional Chinese official political discourse, there was no concept similar to the modern nation-state in Europe. The Chinese regime was often referred to as Jiangshan Sheji (literally: Rivers, Mountains, Earth, and Grains)" in the official documents and in the bureaucratic system. It indicates the land and the people who worked on it to produce the material foundation for sustaining the regime. For the Chinese empire, there was also a political-cultural concept of "all under Heaven," referring to the realm under the emperor's control and wherever the official political and moral values were accepted. The center of "all under Heaven" was "*chaoting*," which literally means the "dynastic court," where the highest political authority resided. The emperor appeared as the Son of Heaven, ruling "all under Heaven."

However, Confucianism was never recognized as a unique element in the national and cultural identity of the Chinese. Only in recent years, perhaps in the past decade, has a strong youth movement appeared to make Confucianism a larger part of the cultural identity of the Han Chinese nationality within and beyond China.[139] Some scholars suggest that this is a revival movement for Confucianism. It was launched by a generation of Han Chinese youth who were cut from the traditions of their ancestors. The doctrines, classics, rites, and way of life (especially the wearing of traditional robes and garments) they adopted as they tried to promote and advocate for Confucianism seem to be reinvented or reconstructed and are lacking social, cultural, and historical contexts. This movement should be understood as one of the responses from the masses for filling in some of the space left by the collapse of the old ideology under the Chinese Communist state since 1989. In other words, Confucianism as a national religion or a national cultural identity could be regarded as a modern and contemporary social construction.

---

[139] K. Carrico, *The Great Han: Race, Nationalism, and Tradition in China Today* (Berkeley: University of California Press, 2017).

Nevertheless, in general, the study of Confucianism and religious life gave birth to the rise of the modern study of Chinese religions in the West. Many issues such as hell, the afterlife, birth and rebirth, gods, and eschatology have continued to appear as the focus of Western-language scholarship to today, which dramatically illustrates a Christian legacy. Arguably, they may or may not be the core issues for the religious life in China.

Bibliography

Adam, R. (1808). *The Religious World Displayed, or A View of the Four Grand Systems of Religion, Judaism, Paganism, Christianity and Mohammedanism; And of the Various Existing Denominations, Sects and Parties, in the Christian World; to Which Is Subjoined, a View of Deism and Atheism.* Edinburgh: Printed by James Ballantyne for Longman, Hurst, Rees, and Orme.

Ahn, D. S. (2011). The Term Question in China: The Theological Factors behind the Translation of Shangti as the Term for "God" in the Chinese Bible in the Nineteenth Century. In P. 'Iolana and S. Tongue eds., *Testing the Boundaries: Self, Faith, Interpretation and Changing Trends in Religious Studies.* Newcastle upon Tyne: Cambridge Scholars Publishing, 95–114.

Alexander, G. G. (1890). *Confucius, the Great Teacher: A Study.* London: Kegan Paul, Trench, and Trübner.

Allsen, T. T. (2004). *Culture and Conquest in Mongol Eurasia.* Cambridge: Cambridge University Press.

Almond, P. C. (1988). *The British Discovery of Buddhism.* Cambridge: Cambridge University Press.

Ashiwa, Y. and Wank D. L. eds. (2009). *Making Religion, Making the State: The Politics of Religion in Modern China.* Stanford: Stanford University Press.

Balfour, F. H. (1881). *The Divine Classic of Nanhua, Being the Works of Chuang Tzse, Taoist Philosopher.* Shanghai: Kelly and Walsh.

Ball, J. D. (1906). *The Celestial and His Religions or the Religious Aspect of China.* Hong Kong: Kelley & Walsh Co.

Barrett, T. H. (2005). Chinese Religion in English Guise: The History of an Illusion. *Modern Asian Studies*, 39(3), 509–533.

Bashford, J. W. (1919). *China: An Interpretation.* New York: The Abingdon Press.

Beal, S. (1884). *Si-yu-ki: Buddhist Record of the Western World.* 2 vols. London: Trübner.

Bettany, G. T. (1891). *Primitive Religions, Being an Introduction to the Study of Religions, with an Account of the Religious Beliefs of Uncivilised Peoples, Confucianism, Taoism (China), and Shintoism (Japan).* London: Ward, Lock, and Bowden.

Bokenkamp, S. R. (2020). *A Fourth-Century Daoist Family: The Zhen'gao, Or Declarations of the Perfected.* vol. 1. Berkeley: University of California Press.

Boone, W. J. (1848). *An Essay on the Proper Rendering of the Words Elohim and Theos into the Chinese Language*. Canton: The Chinese Repository, v.

Boyce, M. (1989). *A History of Zoroastrianism: The Early Period*. Leiden: Brill.

Boyce, M. and Grenet, F. (1991). *A History of Zoroastrianism*. vol. 3. Leiden: Brill.

Boyce, M. and de Jong, A. (2010). *A History or Zoroastrianism*. vol. 4. Leiden: Brill.

Brinkley, F. (1902). *China: Its History, Arts, and Literature*. Boston and Tokyo: J. B. Millet Company.

Brockley, L. M. (2007). *Journey to the East: The Jesuit Mission to China, 1579–1724*. Cambridge, MA: Harvard University Press.

Carrico, K. (2017). *The Great Han: Race, Nationalism, and Tradition in China Today*. Berkeley: University of California Press.

Cawley, K. N. (2013). De-constructing the Name(s) of God: Matteo Ricci's Translational Apostolate. *Translation Studies*, 6(3), 293–308.

Chalmers, J. (1879). Chinese Natural Theology. In V. De Rosen ed., *Travaux de la Troisième session du Congrès International des Orientalistes, St Pétersbourg, 1876*. Tome deuxième. Leiden: E. J. Brill, 15–39.

Chen, H. (2020). Shared Issues in a Shared Textual Community: Buddhism, Christianity and Daoism in Medieval China. In S. N. C. Lieu and G. Thompson eds., *The Church of the East in Central Asia and China*. Turnhout: Brepols, 93–109.

Chen, H. (2006). The Connection between Nestorian and Buddhist Texts in Late Tang China. In R. Malek ed., *The Church of the East in China and Central Asia*. Sankt Augustin: Institut Monumenta Serica, 93–113.

Chen, I. H. (2016). From God's Chinese Names to a Cross-Cultural Universal God: James Legge's Intertextual Theology in His Translation of Tian, Di and Shangdi. *Translation Studies*, 9(3), 268–281.

Chen, S. (1970). *Zhong'ou wenhua jiaoliu shishi luncong* [Collected Papers on the History of the Cultural Exchanges between China and Europe]. Taipei: Shangwu yinshuguan.

Chester, S. H. (1899). *Lights and Shadows of Mission Work in the Far East: Being the Record of Observation Made during a Visit to the Southern Presbyterian Missions in Japan, China, and Korea in the Year of 1897*. Richmond: The Presbyterian Committee of Publication.

Chiang, Y. (2001). *Social Engineering and the Social Sciences in China, 1919–1949*. New York: Cambridge University Press.

The Chinese Recorder and Missionary Journal. vols. 3–37. Shanghai: American Presbyterian Mission Press, 1870–1906.

The Chinese Repository. vols. 1–20. 1832–51. Edited by Elijah Coleman Bridgman and Samuel Wells Williams. Reprinted by Maruzen, Tokyo.

Clark, K. J. and Winslett, J. (2023). *A Spiritual Geography of Early Chinese Thought: Gods, Ancestors, and Afterlife*. London: Bloomsbury Academic.

Clarke, G. W. (1886). The Introduction of Mahometanism into China, *The Chinese Recorder and Missionary Journal*, June, 269–271; August, 294–296.

Cohen, P. A. (1961). The Anti-Christian Tradition in China. *Journal of Asian Studies*, 20(2), 169–180.

Collie, D. (1828). *The Chinese Classical Work Commonly Called the Four Books*. Translated and illustrated with Notes. Malacca: Printed at the Mission Press.

Cordier, H. (1892). *Half a Decade of Chinese Studies, 1886–1891*. Leiden: E. J. Brill.

Davis, E. L. (2001). *Society and the Supernatural in Song China*. Honolulu: University of Hawaii Press.

Dean, K. (1993). *Taoist Ritual and Popular Cults of Southeast China*. Princeton: Princeton University Press.

Dean, W. (1859). *The Chinese Mission. Embracing a History of the Various Missions of all Denominations among the Chinese: With Biographical Sketches of Deceased Missionaries*. New York: Sheldon.

De Groot, J. J. M. (1892–1910). *The Religious System of China, Its Ancient Forms, Evolution, History and Present Aspect, Manners, Customs and Social Institutions Connected Therewith*. 6 volumes. Leiden: Brill.

De Groot, J. J. M. (1912). *Religion in China. Universalism: A Key to the Study of Taoism and Confucianism*. G. P. Putnam's Sons, New York and London: The Knickerbocker Press.

Doré, H. (1911–1938). *Recherches sur les Superstitions* en Chine. 18 vols. Shanghai. Translated by D. J. Finn; v. 13 translated by L. F. McGreal. Reprinted in n 1966, Ch'eng-wen Pub. Co., Taipei.

DuBose, H. C. (1905). Taoism. In E. H. Richards (Ed.), *Religions of Mission Fields as Viewed by Protestant Missionaries* (pp. 161–181). New York: Student Volunteer Movement for Foreign Missions.DuBose, H. C. (1886). *Dragon, Image, and the Demon: Or the Three Religions of China, Confucianism, Buddhism, and Taoism, Giving an Account of the Mythology, Idolatry, and Demonolatry of the Chinese*. London: S. W. Partridge, 1886; New York: A. C. Armstrong, 1887, reprinted.

Dubs, H. H. (1959). Theism and Naturalism in Ancient Chinese Philosophy. *Philosophy East and West*, 9(3–4), 163–172.

Eber, I. (1999). The Interminable Term Question. In I. Eber, S. Wan, and K. Walf in collaboration with R. Malek eds., *Bible in Modern China: The Literary and Intellectual Impact*. Monumenta Serica Monograph series XLIII. Sankt Augustin: Institut Monumenta Serica, in cooperation with the Harry S. Truman Research Institute for the Advancement of Peace, The Hebrew University of Jerusalem. Nettetal: Steyler Verlag, 135–161.

Edkins, J. R. (1863). *Chinese Scenes and People, with Notices of Christian Mission and Missionary Life in a Series of Letters from Various Parts of China, with a Narrative of a Visit to Nanking by Her husband the Rev. Joseph Edkins, also a Memoir by Her Father the Rev. William Stobbs, Stromness*, London: James Nisbet.

Edkins, J. (1893). *The Early Spread of Religious Ideas: Especially in the Far East*. London: The Religious Tract Society.

Edkins, J. (1884/1893). *Religion in China: Containing a Brief Account of the Three Religions of the Chinese: With Observations on the Prospects of Christian Conversion amongst that People*. London: Trübner, Ludgate Hill.

Edkins, J. (1887). The Evolution of the Chinese Language as Exemplifying the Origin and Growth of Human Speech. *Journal of Peking Oriental Society*, 2(1), 1–91.

Edkins, J. (1886). Religious Sects in North China. *The Chinese Recorder and Missionary Journal*, 17(7), 245–252.

Edkins, J. (1880). *Chinese Buddhism: A Volume of Sketches, Historical, Descriptive and Critical*. London: Kegan Paul, Trench, and Trübner.

Edkins, J. (1859). *The Religious Condition of the Chinese: With Observations on the Prospects of Christian Conversion amongst that People*. London: Routledge, Warners & Routledge.

Eitel, E. J. (1870). *Handbook for the Student of Chinese Buddhism*. London: Trübner.

Eitel, E. J. (1871). *Three Lectures on Buddhism*. Hong Kong: At the London Mission House, and London: Trübner.

Faber, E. (1875). *A Systematical Digest of the Doctrines of Confucius, according to the Analects, Great Learning, and Doctrine of the Mean, with an Introduction on the Authorities upon Confucius and Confucianism*. Translated from the German by P. G. von Möllendorff. Hong Kong: Printed at the "China Mail" Office.

Faber, E. (1902). *Chronological Handbook of the History of China*. A Manuscript left by the late Rev. Ernst Faber. Edited by Pastor Paul Kranz. Shanghai: Published by the General Evangelical Protestant Missionary Society of Germany, printed at the American Presbyterian Mission Press.

Faber, E. (1879). *Introduction to the Science of Chinese Religion: A Critique of Max Müller & Other Authors.* Hong Kong: Lane, Crawford.

Faber, E. (1897). *The Mind of Mencius, or Political Economy Founded upon Moral Philosophy. A Systematic Digest of the Doctrines of the Chinese Philosopher Mencius, B.C. 325.* The Original Text Classified and Translated, with Notes and Explanations by the Rev. E. Faber. Second edition translated from the German and Revised by the Rev. A. B. Hutchinson, Tokyo: Nippon Seikokwai Shuppan Kwaisha, Yokohawa, Shanghai, Hong Kong, Singapore: Kelley and Walsh Limited.

Foltz, R. C. (1999). *Religions of the Silk Road: Premodern Patterns of Globalization.* New York: St. Martin's Press.

Forte, A. (1995). *The Hostage an Shigao and His Offspring: An Iranian Family in China.* Kyoto: Italian School of East Asian Studies.

Fortune, R. (1847/2001). *Three Years Wanderings in the Northern Provinces of China.* London: John Murray, 1847, 2nd ed.; London, New York, Bahrain: Kegan Paul, 2001, reprinted edition.

Gardner, D. (1995). Ghosts and Spirits in the Sung Neo-Confucian World: Chu Hsi on Kuei-shen. *Journal of the American Oriental Society,* 115(4), 598–611.

Gernet, J. (1985). *China and the Christian Impact.* Trans. by Janet Lloyd. Cambridge: Cambridge University Press.

Giles, H. A. (1905). *Religions of Ancient China.* London: Archibald Constable.

Gillman, I. and Klimkeit, H.-J. (1999). *Christians in Asia before 1500.* Ann Arbor: University of Michigan Press.

Girardot, N. J. (2002). *The Victorian Translation of China: James Legge's Oriental Pilgrimage.* Berkeley: University of California Press.

Godwin, R. T. (2018). *Persian Christians at the Chinese Court: The Xi'an Stele and the Early Medieval Church of the East.* London: I. B. Taurus.

Granet, M. (1922). *La religion des Chinois.* Paris: Gauthier-Villars & Cie.

Granet, M. (1975). *The Religion of the Chinese People.* Translated, edited and with an introduction by Maurice Freedman. Oxford: Basil Blackwell.

Gray, J. H. (1878/2002). *China: A History of the Law, Manners, and Customs of the People.* London: Macmillan, 1878; Mineola: Dover, 2002, reprinted.

Grenet, F. (2007). Religious Diversity among Sogdian Merchants in Sixth-Century China: Zoroastrianism, Buddhism, Manichaeism, and Hinduism. *Comparative Studies of South Asia, Africa and the Middle East,* 27(2), 463–478.

Grenet, F. (1986). L'art zoroastrien en Sogdiane: études d'iconographie funéraire. *Mesopotamia,* 21, 97–131.

Grenet, F. and Zhang, G. (1998). The Last Refuge of the Sogdian Religion: Dunhuang in the Ninth and Tenth Centuries. *Bulletin of the Asia Institute*, 10, Studies in Honor of Vladimir Livshits, 175–186.

Harrison, H. (2013). *The Missionary's Curse and Other Tales from a Chinese Catholic Village*. Berkeley: University of California Press.

Heyndrickx, J. ed. (1994). *Historiography of the Chinese Catholic Church: Nineteenth and Twentieth Centuries*. Leuven: Ferdinand Verbiest Foundation, K. U. Leuven.

Holloway, K. (2008). *Guodian: The Newly Discovered Seeds of Chinese Religious and Political Philosophy*. Oxford: Oxford University Press.

Huang, J. X. (2001). *Shengxian yu shengtu: lishi yu zongjiao lunwenji* 聖賢與聖徒:歷史與宗教論文集 [Sages and Saints: Collected Papers on History and Religions]. Taipei: Yuncheng wenhua chuban gongsi.

Huang, J. X. (1994). *Youru shengyu: quanli, xinyang yu zhengdangxing* 優入聖域:權力、信仰與正當性 [Ascending the Holy Realm: Power, Belief, and Legitimacy]. Taipei: Yuncheng wenhua chuban gongsi.

Hunter, E. C. D. (2009). The Persian Contribution to Christianity in China: Reflections in the Xian Fu Syriac Inscriptions. In D. W. Winkler and L. Tang eds., *Hidden Treasures and Intercultural Encounters: Studies on East Syriac Christianity in Central Asia and China*. Berlin: Lit; London: Global, 71–86.

Hymes, R. (2002). *Way and Byway: Taoism, Local Religion, and Models of Divinity in Sung and Modern China*. Berkeley: University of California Press.

Jao, T. (1984). Lun Qiyao Yu Shiyiyao [On Seven Stars and Eleven Stars: On Kang Zun's Commentary on Daily Book from 974]. In *Xuantang jilin*, Taipei: Mingwen shuju, 771–793.

Jensen, L. M. (1998). *Manufacturing Confucianism: Chinese Traditions and Universal Civilization*. Durham: Duke University Press.

Ji, J. (2007). *Encounters between Chinese Culture and Christianity: A Hermeneutical Perspective*. Berlin and Münster: LIT Verlag.

Johnson, S. (1872–1885). *Oriental Religions and Their Relation to Universal Religion*. 3 vols. Boston: Houghton, Oswoord.

Johnston, A. (2003). *Missionary Writing and Empire: 1800–1860*. Cambridge: Cambridge University Press.

Johnston, J. (1897). *China and Formosa: The Story of the Mission of the Presbyterian Church of England*. London: Harzell, Watson, & Viney, Ld.

Jordan, L. H. (1905). *Comparative Religion: Its Genesis and Growth*. Edinburgh: T. and T. Clark.

Katz, P. (2000). *Images of the Immortal: The Cult of Lu Dongbin at the Palace of Eternal Joy*. Honolulu: University of Hawaii Press.

Kellogg, S. H. (1899). *A Handbook of Comparative Religion*. Philadelphia: The Westminster Press.

Kellogg, S. H. (1885). *The Light of Asia and the Light of the World, A Comparison of the Legend, the Doctrine, & the Ethics of the Buddha with the Story, the Doctrine, & the Ethics of Christ*. London: Macmillan.

Kidd, S. (1841). *China, or Illustrations of the Symbols, Philosophy, Antiquities, Customs, Superstitions, Law, Government, Education, and Literature of the Chinese*. London: Taylor & Walton.

Kindopp, J. and Hemrin, C. L. eds. (2004). *God and Caesar in China: Policy Implications of Church-State Tensions*. Washington, DC: Brookings Institution Press.

King, R. (1999). *Orientalism and Religion: Post-Colonial Theory, India and "The Mystic East."* London: Routledge.

Kippenberg, H. G. (2002). *Discovering Religious History in the Modern Age*. Princeton: Princeton University Press.

Kuenen, A. (1882). *National Religions and Universal Religions*. Hibbert Lectures, 1882. Translated by P. H. Wicksteed. London: Macmillan.

Lagerway, J. (1987). *Taoist Ritual in Chinese Society and History*. New York: Macmillan.

Lee, J. T. (2003). *The Bible and the Gun: Christianity in South China, 1860–1900*. London and New York: Routledge.

Legge, J. (1886). *A Record of the Buddhist Kingdoms, being an Account by the Chinese Monk Fa-hsien and his Travels in India and Ceylon (AD 399–414) in Search of the Buddhist Books of Discipline*. Translated and annotated by James Legge. Oxford: Clarendon Press.

Legge, J. (1850). *An Argument for Shang-te as the Proper Rendering of the Words Elohim and Theos, In the Chinese Language; with Strictures on the Essay of Bishop Boone in Favour of the Term Shin, etc.*, Hong Kong: The Hong Kong Register Office.

Legge, J. (1888). *Christianity in China: Nestorianism, Roman Catholicism, Protestantism*. London: Trübner.

Legge, H. E. (1905). *James Legge: Missionary and Scholar*. London: The Religious Tract Society.

Legge, J. (1891). *The Sacred Books of China: The Texts of Taoism*. Translated by James Legge. Oxford: The Clarendon Press.

Legge, J. (1879). *The Sacred Books of China: The Texts of Confucianism*. Translated by James Legge. Oxford: Clarendon Press.

Legge, J. (1852). *The Notions of the Chinese Concerning God and Spirits: With an Examination of the Defenses of an Essay, on the Proper Rendering of the*

Words Elohim and Theos, into the Chinese Language. Hong Kong: The Hong Kong Register Office.

Lerner, J. A (2005). Aspects of Assimilation: The Funerary Practices and Furnishings of Central Asians in China. *Sino-Platonic Papers*, 168, 1–65.

Lerner, J. A. (2011). Zoroastrian Funerary Beliefs and Practices Known from the Sino-Sogdian Tombs in China. *The Silk Road*, 9, 18–25.

Li, Ji. (2015). *God's Little Daughters: Catholic Women in Nineteenth-Century Manchuria*. Seattle: University of Washington Press.

Lian, X. (1997). *The Conversion of Missionaries: Liberalism in American Protestant Missions in China, 1907–1932*. University Park, PA: Pennsylvania State University Press.

Lieu, S. N. C. (1998). *Manichaeism in Central Asia and China*. Leiden: Brill.

Lieu, S. N. C. (1985). *Manichaeism in the Later Roman Empire and Medieval China: A Historical Survey*. Manchester: Manchester University Press.

Lillegard, G. (1929). *The Chinese Term Question: An Analysis of the Problem and Historical Sketch of the Controversy*. Boston: Christian Book Room.

Lilly, W. S. (1885). *Ancient and Modern Thought*. London: Chapman and Hall.

Lin, W. (1995). *Bosi baihuojiao yu gudai Zhongguo* (Zoroastrianism and Ancient China). Taipei: Xinwenfeng chuban gongsi.

Liu, S. (1978). Theism from a Chinese Perspective. *Philosophy East and West*, 28(4), 413–417.

Liu, Y. (2014). Adapting Catholicism to Confucianism: Matteo Ricci's *Tianzhu Shiyi*. *The European Legacy*, 19(1), 43–59.

Loewe, M. (1988). The Jewish Presence in Imperial China. *Jewish Historical Studies*, 30, 1–20.

Lutz, J. G. (1976). Chinese Nationalism and the Anti-Christian Campaigns of the 1920s. *Modern Asian Studies*, 10(3), 395–416.

MacKenzie, D. N. (1976). *The Buddhist Sogdian Texts of the British Library*. Acta Iranica 10. Téhéran: Bibliothèque Pahlavi; Leiden: Diffusion, Brill.

MacKenzie, D. N. (1970). *The "Sūtra of the Causes and Effects of Actions" in Sogdian*. London: School of Oriental and African Studies, University of London.

Malan, S. C. (1855). *Who Is God in China, Shin or Shang-Te? Remarks on the Etymology of Theos and Elohim and on the Rendering of Those Terms into Chinese*. London: S. Bagster.

Malandra, W. W. (1983). *An Introduction to Ancient Iranian Religion: Readings from the Avesta and Achaemenid Inscriptions*. Minneapolis: University of Minnesota Press.

Malek, R. ed. (2006). *Jingjiao: The Church of the East in China and Central Asia*. Monumenta Serica Institute, Sankt Augustin, Nettetal: Steyler Verlag.

Marshak, B. I. (2004). The Sarcophagus of Sabao Yu Hong: A Head of the Foreign Merchants (592–598). *Orientations*, 35, 57–65.

Marshak, B. I. (2001). La thématique sogdienne dans l'art de la Chine de la seconde moitié du VIe siècle. *Comptes rendus des séances de l'année 2001*, Paris: Académie des inscriptions et belles-lettres, 227–264.

Martin, W. A. P. (1880). *Hanlin Paper or Essays on the Intellectual Life of the Chinese*. London: Trübner and Shanghai: Kelley & Walsh Limited.

Martin, W. A. P. (1890). The Worship of Ancestors – A Plea for Toleration. In the Editorial Committee ed., *Records of the General Conference of the Protestant Missionaries in China, Held at Shanghai, May 7–20, 1890*. Shanghai: American Presbyterian Mission Press, 619–631.

Martin, W. A. P. (1881). *The Chinese, Their Education, Philosophy and Letters*. New York: Harper and Brothers.

Masuzawa, T. (2005). *The Invention of World Religions: Or, How European Universalism Was Preserved in the Language of Pluralism*. Chicago: University of Chicago Press.

Matheson, D. (1866). *Narrative of the Mission to China of the English Presbyterian Church. With Remarks on the Social Life and Religious Ideas of the Chinese by the Rev. John MacGowan, and Notes on Climate, Health, and Outfit, by John Carnegie*. London: James Nisbet.

Maurice, F. D. (1847). *The Religions of the World and Their Relations to Christianity, Considered in Eight Lectures Founded by the Right Hon. Robert Boyle*. London: John W. Parker.

McRae, J. and Nattier, J. eds. (1999). *Buddhism across Boundaries: Chinese Buddhism and the Western Regions*. Sanchung: Fo Guang Shan Foundation.

Meadows, T. T. (1856). *The Chinese and Their Rebellions, Viewed in Connection with Their National Philosophy, Ethics, Legislation, and Administration*. London: Smith, Older.

Medhurst, W. H. (1847). *An Inquiry into the Proper Mode of Rendering the Word God in Translating the Sacred Scriptures into the Chinese Language*. Shanghai: The Mission Press.

Meynard, T. (2011). Chinese Buddhism and the Threat of Atheism in Seventeenth-Century Europe. *Buddhist-Christian Studies*, 31, 3–23.

Milne, W. (1820). *A Retrospect of the First Ten Years of Protestant Mission in China, Accompanied with Miscellaneous Remarks on the Literature, History, and Mythology of China, etc.* Malacca: The Anglo-Chinese Press.

Moffat, J. C. (1889). *A Comparative History of Religions: Before Christ. Part I: Ancient Scriptures*. New edition revised. New York: Dodd, Mead.

Morison, J. (1844). *The Father and Founders of the London Missionary Society: A Jubilee Memorial Including a Sketch of the Origin and*

Progress of the Institution, a New Edition with Twenty-One Portraits, London: Fisher.

Morrison, R. (1817). *A View of China for Philological Purposes, Containing a Sketch of Chinese Chronology, Geography, Government, Religion & Customs*. Macao: P. P. Thomas.

Morrison, R. (1834). The State Religion of China; Objects of the Governmental Worship; the Ministers or Priests, or the Preparation Required for Their Service; Sacrifices, Offerings, Ceremonies; and Penalties for Informality. *Chinese Repository*, 3(2), 49–53.

Moule, A. E. (1871). *Four Hundred Million: Chapters on China and the Chinese*. London: Seeley, Jackson, & Halliday.

Muirhead, W. (1870). *China and the Gospel*. London: James Nisbet.

Muirhead, W. (1890). Historical Summary of the Different Versions, with Their Terminology, and the Feasibility of Securing a Single Standard Version in Wen-li, with a Corresponding Version in Mandarin Colloquial. In the Editorial Committee ed., *Records of the General Conference of the Protestant Missionaries in China, Held at Shanghai, May 7–20, 1890*, Shanghai: American Presbyterian Mission Press, 33–41.

Muirhead, W. (1879). *Ru shi dao hui yesu wujiao tongkao* [Confucianism, Buddhism, Daoism, Islam, and Christianity: A General Introduction to Five Teachings]. Tokyo: Jujiya.

Müller, F. M. (1889). *Introduction to the Science of Religion*. London: Longmans, Green.

Müller, F. M. (1885). *Lectures on the Science of Language*. London: Longmans, Green, New Edition.

Müller, F. M. (1860). *A History of Ancient Sanskrit Literature So Far as It Illustrates the Primitive Religion of the Brahmans*. London: Williams and Norgate.

Mungello, D. E. (1994). *The Chinese Rites Controversy: Its History and Meaning*. Nettetal: Steyler and Sankt Augustin: Institut Monumenta Serica.

Needham, J. (1959). *Science and Civilization in China*. vol. 3: Mathematics and the Sciences of the Heavens and the Earth. Cambridge: Cambridge University Press.

Nevius, J. L. (1869). *China and the Chinese: A General Description of the Country and Its Inhabitants; its Civilization and Form of Government; Its Religious and Social Institutions; Its Intercourse with Other Nations; and Its Present Condition and Prospects*. New York: Harper & Brothers.

Nicolini-Zani, M. (2022). *The Luminous Way to the East: Texts and History of the First Encounter of Christianity with China*. Oxford: Oxford University Press.

Owen, G. (1900). The Outlook in China. *The Chronicle of London Missionary Society*, (9), 107; new series, 31–32.

Parker, E. H. (1905). *China and Religion*. New York: E. P. Dutton.

Pelliot, P. (1996). *L'inscription nestorienne de Si-ngan-fu*, Edited with Supplements by A. Forte. Kyoto: Scuola di Studi sul l'Asie Orientale, Paris: College de France, Institut des Hautes Etudes Chinoises.

Pfister, L. F. (2010). Bible Translations and the Protestant "Term Question." In R. G. Tiedemann ed., *Handbook of Christianity in China*. volume 2: 1800–present. Leiden: Brill, 361–370.

Pfister, L. F. (2004). *Striving for "The Whole Duty of Man": James Legge and the Scottish Protestant Encounter with China. Assessing Confluences in Scottish Nonconformism, Chinese Missionary Scholarship, Victorian Sinology, and Chinese Protestantism*. Frankfurt and Main: Peter Lang.

Pieragastini, S. (2018). Jesuit and Protestant Encounters in Jiangnan: Contest and Cooperation in China's Lower Yangzi Region. In J. Cañizares-Esguerra, R. A. Maryks, and R. P. Hsia eds., *Encounters between Jesuits and Protestants in Asia and the Americas*. Leiden: Brill, 117–136.

Poo, M. (1998). *In Search of Personal Welfare: A View of Ancient Chinese Religion*. Albany: State University of New York Press.

Puett, M. (2004). *To Become a God: Cosmology, Sacrifice, and Self-Divination in Early China*. Cambridge, MA: Harvard University Press.

Riboud, P. (2006). La diffusion des religions du monde iranien en Chine entre le VIe et le Xe siècle de notre ère. *Etudes Chinoises*, 24, 269–284.

Richard, T. (1916). *Forty-Five Years in China: Reminiscences by Timothy Richard*. New York: Frederick A. Stokes Company.

Roberts, J. S. (1878). Principles of Translation into Chinese. In the Editorial Committee, *Records of the General Conference of the Protestant Missionaries of China held at Shanghai, May 10–24, 1877*. Shanghai: Presbyterian Mission Press.

Robinet, I. (1979). *Taoist Meditation: The Mao-Shan Tradition of Great Purity*. Translated by Julian F. Pas, Norman J. Girardot. Albany: State University of New York Press.

Rong, X. (2001). Yi ge shi Tangchao de Bosi Jingjiao jiazu [A Nestorian Christian Family Who Served in the Tang Government]. In *Zhonggu Zhongguo yu wailai wenming* (Medieval China and Foreign Civilizations). Beijing: Sanlian shudian, 238–257.

Rose, J. (2000). *The Image of Zoroaster: The Persian Mage through European Eyes*. Ann Arbor: University of Michigan Press.

De Rosen, V. ed. (1879). *Travaux de la Troisième session du Congrès International des Orientalistes, St Pétersbourg, 1876.* Tome deuxième. Leiden: E. J. Brill.

Ross, J. (1909). *The Original Religion of China.* Edinburgh and London: Oliphant Anderson & Ferrier.

Rowell, G. (1874). *Hell and the Victorians: A Study of the Nineteenth-Century Theological Controversies Concerning Eternal Punishment and the Future Life.* Oxford: Clarendon Press.

Saeki, Y. (1951). *The Nestorian Documents and Relics in China.* Tokyo: The Toho Bunkawa Gakuin: The Academy of Oriental Culture, Tokyo Institute, The Maruzen.

Secrist, H. T. (1909). *Comparative Studies in Religion: An Introduction to Unitarianism.* Boston: Unitarian Sunday-School Society.

Shahar, M. (2008). *Oedipal God: The Chinese Nezha and his Indian Origins.* Honolulu: University of Hawai'i Press.

Sheffield, D. Z. (1905). Confucianism. In *Religions of Mission Fields as Viewed by Protestant Missionaries.* New York: Student Volunteer Movement for Foreign Missions, 183–211.

Sheffield, D. Z. (1886). The Ethics of Christianity and of Confucianism Compared. *The Chinese Recorder and Missionary Journal,* 17(10), 365–379.

Sims-Williams, N. (1992). Sogdian and Turkish Christians in the Turfan and Tun-huang Manuscripts. In A. Cadonna ed., *Turfan and Tun-huang the Texts: Encounter of Civilization on the Silk Road.* Firenze: Leo S. Olschki, 43–61.

Sirr, H. C. (1849). *China and the Chinese: Their Religion, Character, Customs, and Manufactures, the Evils Arising from the Opium Trade, with a Glance of Our Religious, Moral, and Commercial Intercourse with the Country.* London: Wm. S. Orr.

Slingerland, E. (2018). *Mind and Body in Early China: Beyond Orientalism and the Myth of Holism.* Oxford: Oxford University Press.

Smith, G. (1847). *A Narrative of an Exploratory Visit to Each of the Consular Cities of China and to the Islands of Hong Kong and Chushan, in behalf of the Church Missionary Society, in the years 1844, 1845, 1846.* New York: Happer & Brothers.

Smith, A. H. (1907). *The Uplift of China,* New York: Young People's Missionary Movement.

Smith, A. H. (1899). *Village Life in China: A Study in Sociology.* New York: Fleming H. Revell Company, Publishers for Evangelical Literature.

Song, G. (2018). *Giulio Aleni, Kouduo Richao, and Christian–Confucian Dialogism in Late Ming Fujian.* London: Routledge.

Soothill, W. E. (1907). *A Mission in China*. Edinburgh and London: Oliphant, Anderson & Ferrier.

Soothill, W. E. (1924). *Timothy Richard of China: Seer, Statesman, Missionary & the Most Disinterested Adviser the Chinese Ever Had*. London: Seeley, Service.

Soothill, W. E. (1913). *The Three Religions of China*. London: Hodder and Stroughton.

Spelman, D. G. (1969). Christianity in Chinese: The Protestant Term Question. *Papers on China*, 22A, East Asian Research Center, Harvard University, 25–52.

Standaert, N. (1988). *Yang Tingyun, Confucian and Christian in Late Ming China: His Life and Thought*. Leiden: Brill.

Strickmann, M. (2002). *Chinese Magical Medicine*. Stanford: Stanford University Press.

Strickmann, M. (1977). The Mao Shan Revelations: Taoism and the Aristocracy. *T'oung Pao* 2nd Series, 63(1), 1–64.

Stroumsa, G. G. (2010). *A New Science: The Discovery of Religion in the Age of Reason*. Cambridge, MA: Harvard University Press.

Sun, A. (2013). *Confucianism as a World Religion: Contested Histories and Contemporary Realities*. Princeton: Princeton University Press.

Tang, L. (2002). *A Study of the History of Nestorian Christianity in China and Its Literature in Chinese: Together with a New English Translation of the Dunhuang Nestorian Documents*. Frankfurt/M: Peter Lang.

Teiser, S. F. (2018). Introduction: The Spirits of Chinese Religion. In D. S. Lopez ed., *Religions of Asia in Practice: An Anthology*. Princeton: Princeton University Press, 295–329.

The Conference Committee, (1907). *China Centenary Missionary Conference Records: Report of the Great Conference Held at Shanghai, April 5 to May 8, 1907*. New York: American Tract Society, Printed in Shanghai.

The Editorial Committee, ed. (1878). *Records of the General Conference of the Protestant Missionaries of China, Held at Shanghai, May 10–24, 1877*. Shanghai: Presbyterian Mission Press.

The Tract Committee, ed. (1891). *Church Work in North China; being A Sketch of the Church of England Mission in North China, together with an Account of the Formation of the Diocese*. With a Preface by the Right Rev. C. P. Scott. London: Society for Promoting Christian Knowledge.

Tiedemann, R. G. ed. (2010). *Handbook of Christianity in China*. vol. 2: 1800 to the Present. Leiden: Brill.

Tiele, C. P. (1877). *Outlines of the History of Religion to the Spread of the Universal Religions*. Translated by J. Estlin Carpenter. London: Kegan Paul, Trench, Trübner.

Tillman, H. C. (1992). *Confucian Discourse and Chu Hsi's Ascendancy*. Honolulu: University of Hawai'i Press.

Turner, J. A. (1894). *Kwang Tung or Five Years in South China*. London: S. W. Partridge, 1894; Hong Kong: Oxford University Press, 1982, reprinted.

von Glahn, R. (2004). *The Sinister Way: The Divine and the Demonic in Chinese Religious Culture*. Berkeley: University of California Press.

Walter, M. N. (2006). Sogdians and Buddhism. *Sino-Platonic Papers*, 174.

Walter, M. N. (1998). Tokharian Buddhism in Kucha: Buddhism of Indo-European Centum Speakers in Chinese Turkestan before the 10th Century C.E. *Sino-Platonic Papers*, 85.

Watson, J. (1985). Standardizing the Gods: The Promotion of T'ien Hou Along the South China Coast, 960–1960. In D. Johnson, A. J. Nathan, and E. S. Rawski eds., *Popular Culture in Late Imperial China*. Berkeley: University of California Press, 292–324.

Wei, S. L. (2018). Jesuit and Protestant Use of Vernacular Chinese in Accommodation Policy. In J. Cañizares-Esguerra, R. A. Maryks, and R. P. Hsia eds., *Encounters between Jesuits and Protestants in Asia and the Americas*. Leiden: Brill, 73–89.

Williams, S. W. (1848). *The Middle Kingdom: A Survey of the Geography, Government, Education, Social Life, Arts, Religion, & of the Chinese Empire and Its Inhabitants*. New York and London: Wiley and Putnam.

Williams, S. W. (1878). The Controversy among the Protestant Missionaries on the Proper Translation of the Words God and Spirit into the Chinese. *Bibliotheca Sacra*, 35, 732–778.

Williamson, A. (1870). *Journeys in North China, Manchuria, and Eastern Mongolia, with Some Account of Corea*. London: Smith, Elder.

Wilson, T. A. (2002). Culture, Society, Politics, and the Cult of Confucius. In T. A. Wilson, ed., *On Sacred Grounds: Culture, Society, Politics, and the Formation of the Cult of Confucius*. Cambridge, MA: Center for Asian Studies, Harvard University, 1–40.

Wilson, T. A. (2002). Sacrifice and the Imperial Cult of Confucius. *History of Religions*, 41(3), 251–287.

Wilson, T. A. (1996). The Ritual Formation of Confucian Orthodoxy and the Descendants of the Sage. *The Journal of Asian Studies*, 55(3), 559–584.

Winterbotham, W. (1795). *An Historical, Geographical, and Philosophical View of the Chinese Empire; Comprehending a Description of the Fifteen Provinces of China, Chinese Tartary, Tributary States, Natural History of*

China, Government, Religion, Laws, Manners and Customs, Literature, Arts, Sciences, Manufactures, & c. London, printed for and sold by the editor, J. Ridgway, and W. Button.

Wolf, A. P. (1978). Gods, Ghosts, and Ancestors. In A. P. Wolf ed., *Religion and Ritual in Chinese Society*. Stanford: Stanford University Press, 131–182.

Wylie, A. (1867). *Memorials of Protestant Missionaries to the Chinese: Giving a List of Their Publications, and Obituary Notices of the Deceased*. Shanghai: American Presbyterian Mission Press.

Yamamoto, T. and Yamamoto, S. (1953). The Anti-Christian Movement in China, 1922–1927. *The Far Eastern Quarterly*, 12(2), 133–147.

Yang, C. K. (1991). *Religion in Chinese Society: A Study of Contemporary Social Functions of Religion and Some of Their Historical Factors*. Prospect Heights: Waveland Press.

Yao, K. X. (2008). At the Turn of the Century: A Study of the China Centenary Missionary Conference of 1907. *International Bulletin of Missionary Research*, 32(2), 65–70.

Young, E. P. (2013). *Ecclesiastical Colony: China's Catholic Church and the French Religious Protectorate*. Oxford: Oxford University Press.

Yü, C. (2001). *Kuan-yin: The Chinese Transformation of Avalokiteśvara*. New York: Columbia University Press.

Zagorin, P. (2003). *How the Idea of Religious Tolerance Came to the West*. Princeton: Princeton University Press.

Zetzsche, J. O. (1999). *The Bible in China: The History of the Union Version or the Culmination of Protestant Missionary Bible Translation in China*. Sankt Augustin: Monumenta Serica Insitut.

Zhang, G. (1997). Revisiting the Zoroastrian Painting in the Tang Dynasty: If the Image Depicted in the Dunhuang Manuscript P. 4518 (24) Can Be Identified as Zoroastrian Deities Daēna and Daēva? *Tang Yanjiu* (Journal of Tang Studies), 3, 1–17.

Zhang, G. (1994). Trois exemples d'influences mazdéennes dans la Chine des Tang, *Études Chinoises*, 13(1–2), Mélanges de sinologie offerts à Jacques Gernet, 203–219.

Zhang, X. (2010). *Zhonggu huahua xianjiao kaoshu* [A Study of Sinicized Zoroastrianism in Medieval China]. Beijing: Wenwu chubanshe.

Zürcher, E. (1972). *The Buddhist Conquest of China: The Spread and Adaptation of Buddhism in Early Medieval China*. Leiden: Brill.

Cambridge Elements =

Religion and Monotheism

Paul K. Moser
Loyola University Chicago

Paul K. Moser is Professor of Philosophy at Loyola University Chicago. He is the author of *God in Moral Experience; Paul's Gospel of Divine Self-Sacrifice; The Divine Goodness of Jesus; Divine Guidance; Understanding Religious Experience; The God Relationship; The Elusive God* (winner of national book award from the Jesuit Honor Society); *The Evidence for God; The Severity of God; Knowledge and Evidence* (all Cambridge University Press); and *Philosophy after Objectivity* (Oxford University Press); coauthor of *Theory of Knowledge* (Oxford University Press); editor of *Jesus and Philosophy* (Cambridge University Press) and *The Oxford Handbook of Epistemology* (Oxford University Press); and coeditor of *The Wisdom of the Christian Faith* (Cambridge University Press). He is the coeditor with Chad Meister of the book series *Cambridge Studies in Religion, Philosophy, and Society*.

Chad Meister
*Affiliate Scholar, Ansari Institute for Global Engagement with Religion,
University of Notre Dame*

Chad Meister is Affiliate Scholar at the Ansari Institute for Global Engagement with Religion at the University of Notre Dame. His authored and co-authored books include *Evil: A Guide for the Perplexed* (Bloomsbury Academic, 2nd edition); *Introducing Philosophy of Religion* (Routledge); *Introducing Christian Thought* (Routledge, 2nd edition); and *Contemporary Philosophical Theology* (Routledge). He has edited or co-edited the following: *The Oxford Handbook of Religious Diversity* (Oxford University Press); *Debating Christian Theism* (Oxford University Press); with Paul Moser, *The Cambridge Companion to the Problem of Evil* (Cambridge University Press); and with Charles Taliaferro, *The History of Evil* (Routledge, in six volumes). He is the co-editor with Paul Moser of the book series *Cambridge Studies in Religion, Philosophy, and Society*.

About the Series

This Cambridge Element series publishes original concise volumes on monotheism and its significance. Monotheism has occupied inquirers since the time of the Biblical patriarch, and it continues to attract interdisciplinary academic work today. Engaging, current, and concise, the Elements benefit teachers, researched, and advanced students in religious studies, Biblical studies, theology, philosophy of religion, and related fields.

Cambridge Elements

Religion and Monotheism

Elements in the Series

Jewish Monotheism and Slavery
Catherine Hezser

Open Theism
Alan R. Rhoda

African Philosophy of Religion and Western Monotheism
Kirk Lougheed, Motsamai Molefe and Thaddeus Metz

Monotheism and Pluralism
Rachel S. Mikva

The Abrahamic Vernacular
Rebecca Scharbach Wollenberg

Monotheism and Fundamentalism: Prevalence, Potential, and Resilience
Rik Peels

Emotions and Monotheism
John Corrigan

Monotheism and Peacebuilding
John D Brewer

Monotheism and Wisdom in the Hebrew Bible: An Uneasy Pair?
James L. Crenshaw

Monotheism and Relativism
Bernd Irlenborn

Monotheism and Miracle
Eric Eve

Seeking Monotheism in Chinese Religions
Huaiyu Chen

A full series listing is available at: www.cambridge.org/er&m

For EU product safety concerns, contact us at Calle de José Abascal, 56–1°, 28003 Madrid, Spain or eugpsr@cambridge.org.